Disability Rights

ISSUES
(formerly Issues for the Nineties)

Volume 17

Editor

Craig Donnellan

Independence
Educational Publishers
Cambridge

First published by Independence
PO Box 295
Cambridge CB1 3XP
England

British Library Cataloguing in Publication Data
Disability Rights – (Issues Series)
I. Donnellan, Craig II. Series
362.4

ISBN 1 86168 177 1

Printed in Great Britain
The Burlington Press
Cambridge

Typeset by
Claire Boyd

Cover
The illustration on the front cover is by
Pumpkin House.

CONTENTS

Chapter One: Discrimination

In the dark on disability   1

What is discrimination?   2

Disability awareness   3

Disabled customers   6

Poverty and benefits   7

Benefits for the extra costs of disability   8

Disabled children   10

Disability in the UK   10

Talking my language   11

A role for the disabled   12

Human wrongs   13

Disability discrimination   14

Regional disabled people still
excluded from work   15

Call to give disabled real job opportunities   16

Disability does not mean inability   17

Employment   18

Disability rights to cover millions more workers   19

Disabled people as workers   20

Disabled people and society   20

Left out   22

And the survey shows . . .   24

Disability issues   25

Chapter Two: Learning Disabilities

What is a learning disability?   28

British Institute of Learning Disabilities   29

How many people have learning disabilities?   30

Mencap research points to the
public's double standards   30

Inclusive education   31

Learning disabilities   33

Time to open a new set of doors   34

The neglect of so many disabled pupils
is scandalous   36

'It is not disability but an
attitude problem of others'   36

More money for disabled students   37

Understanding learning disability   37

Special Educational Needs and Disability Bill   38

Scotland puts learning disabilities centre stage   40

Additional resources   41

Index   42

Web site information   43

Acknowledgements   44

Introduction

Disability Rights is the seventeenth volume in the **Issues** series. The aim of this series is to offer up-to-date information about important issues in our world.

Disability Rights examines the discrimination faced by people with disabilities and looks at learning disabilities.

The information comes from a wide variety of sources and includes:
Government reports and statistics
Newspaper reports and features
Magazine articles and surveys
Literature from lobby groups
and charitable organisations.

It is hoped that, as you read about the many aspects of the issues explored in this book, you will critically evaluate the information presented. It is important that you decide whether you are being presented with facts or opinions. Does the writer give a biased or an unbiased report? If an opinion is being expressed, do you agree with the writer?

Disability Rights offers a useful starting-point for those who need convenient access to information about the many issues involved. However, it is only a starting-point. At the back of the book is a list of organisations which you may want to contact for further information.

*****

In the dark on disability

Survey reveals public still ignorant on discrimination issues

By John James

Widespread ignorance about who is covered by the Disability Discrimination Act, and widely differing views of what the public regards as disability, have been revealed in a survey for the disability rights commission.

Only half of 2,000 people questioned had heard of the 1995 law, which aims to protect the rights of disabled people. And of those who were aware of the act, only 48% thought it covered Aids, 52% long-term heart conditions, 50% facial disfigurement and 44% cancer. In fact, it is illegal to discriminate against people with any of these conditions.

Overall, the survey found that many people had a limited notion of the extent and nature of disability. There are some 8.5m disabled people in Britain, but when asked what proportion of them used wheelchairs, 46% of respondents said up to a quarter, and 22% about half. The reality is that fewer than 5% of disabled people use a wheelchair. More encouragingly, the survey findings do show a general recognition that disabled people are not treated fairly by society, with 50% agreeing this is so.

Asked if disabled people should have the same right to vote as the rest of the population, only 1% said they should not. But 17% reckoned there could be occasions when it might be justifiable to treat them less favourably.

> *Only half of 2,000 people questioned had heard of the 1995 law, which aims to protect the rights of disabled people*

Paul Gemmill, the commission's policy director, says the findings show that a majority of the public realises there is still considerable discrimination against disabled people, and a real lack of awareness of their rights under law.

The commission, set up a year ago, does not itself emerge from the survey with a high public recognition rating. Of those questioned last month by BMRB, 76% had not heard of it and only 19% said they had. More alarmingly, 71% of disabled people – one in 10 of the sample – had not heard of it and just 24% were aware of its existence.

In an attempt to raise its profile, the commission is embarking on a series of initiatives – the latest of which is a drive to emphasise the rights of disabled customers. A poster and local advertising campaign has been launched, with supermarkets and travel companies in particular being reminded of their obligations.

The commission has also set up a conciliation service to help settle discrimination disputes between businesses and disabled people without the need to go to court. Bert Massie, who chairs the commission, says: 'We know from thousands of calls to our helpline that disabled people get a raw deal as customers on a daily basis.

'Disabled people have around £40bn a year to spend – a fact that business owners and service providers need to bear in mind.'

© Guardian Newspapers Limited 2001

What is discrimination?

Information from the Disability Rights Commission (DRC)

Discrimination is when you have been treated worse than non-disabled people simply because of your disability, whether it be, for example, in the field of employment or service provision. You might have been turned down for a job or refused insurance because of your disability. An employer or service provider may have made no attempt to change their practices or circumstances – otherwise known as making a 'reasonable adjustment'.

Deciding on your options: what can be done if you have faced disability discrimination?

If you think you have been *discriminated* against because of your disability or health condition, the following 7 points will help you think through what you want to do next.

Was it discrimination?

Ask yourself, was your experience *discrimination* – that is, being treated unfairly ('less favourably' to use the legal jargon) because of your disability? Or was it just plain poor treatment that anyone might have experienced? If you answer 'yes, it was discrimination' move on to the following points. If you answer 'no', but you want to make a complaint to the manager of the business or organisation that treated you badly, they should advise you about their complaints procedure.

What do you want to do about it?

If you think you've faced *discrimination* you might want to try writing or talking to the person or organisation to seek an apology or a change in their behaviour in the future. And/or you might want to know your legal rights. The DRC Helpline (Telephone: 08457 622 633, textphone: 08457 622 644) can help you talk through the options.

Was it illegal?

If the DRC agrees you may have faced discrimination, we can help you work out what to do next. We can advise on whether you may have been treated *illegally*, under the Disability Discrimination Act 1995. Some types of discrimination – unfortunately – are not illegal, for example transport is not fully covered by the Disability Discrimination Act; and not everyone facing discrimination because of their impairment or health condition is covered (it depends on the length of time and the effects of your impairment). The DRC is seeking improvements in the law. The DRC can advise you on whether the law may have been broken. If not, you may want to point out to the organisation that discriminated against you what 'best practice' is – and we can advise you on what other companies in similar circumstances have done and what this particular organisation might do.

If it was illegal, is there a chance of negotiating a solution?

Many employers and providers of services may want to adopt good practice, but are not sure how to do it. In this case, the DRC can advise you on suggestions you might make to them – or we can advise them directly, if you wish. With others, mentioning that you think they may have broken the law can motivate them to seek a resolution – so although you are exercising your legal rights, you may never need actually to take any legal action. A DRS caseworker can investigate the facts

of the case for/with you and then, if you wish, help you to negotiate a settlement.

If the problem can't be easily resolved, would you be interested in conciliation?

Conciliation involves an independent conciliator, who talks to you and the organisation against whom you are complaining, and seeks a solution which both sides can agree to.

If the problem can't be solved through any of these means, or if your case raises legal issues that have never been tested before, do you want to consider legal action?

The DRC can advise you on what would be involved if you decide to take the employer to an Employment Tribunal; or to take a service provider to Court.

If your case of discrimination is one that could help other people understand the problems disabled people face, or the solutions that can be negotiated, would you want to speak about it publicly? Or to have your experience described anonymously?

This is a very personal decision. We neither encourage nor discourage you to share your experience with others. But if you do want to – either anonymously or publicly – we can help you achieve that, by writing up your experience and including it in our bank of examples that we publicise in reports, speeches and the media; or by adding your name to our list of people who may be interested in speaking to a journalist, or researcher. It's your decision.

• The above information is an extract from *Challenging Disability Discrimination – A Guide to Services*, produced by the Disability Rights Commission, 222 Grays-Inn Road London, WC1X 8HL.

Disability awareness

Information from the Disabled Living Foundation (DLF)

Introduction

The Disabled Living Foundation (DLF) is contacted by many people each year studying different aspects of disability as part of their course work or for their own personal development. This article has been written to give some insight into the issues surrounding disability, particularly focusing on the ways disability in today's society continues to be a barrier to achievement and equality.

Disability is prevalent and affects all age groups. The 1988 survey carried out by the Office of Population Censuses and Surveys puts the figure on the number of disabled people in Great Britain at 6.5 million. Disability groups argue that this figure should in fact be much higher; many people have been excluded from the statistics because of the problems of defining disability. Although attitudes towards disabled people and other minority groups within our society are changing and becoming more positive, there still seems to be an immense lack of understanding about disability. There is often an assumption that all disabled people are the same, reinforced by the term 'the disabled' – and how often disabled people seem to be portrayed (particularly in the media) as 'disadvantaged individuals' whose disabilities cause 'suffering'.

However, disabled people have found their voice, particularly through organisations that are set up and run by disabled people, and often referred to as the Disability Movement. Many disabled people would argue that society should not be categorised by what is normal and abnormal – after all, who and what determines the parameters? When does having difficulty walking, for example, qualify an individual for 'disabled' status? Many people will be affected by illnesses or accidents that will cause temporary impairment at some stage in their lives, and therefore inability to carry out

activities in what is considered to be the 'normal' way should be recognised as being part and parcel of everyday life. It is the environment that imposes constraints preventing disabled people from running their lives in a way equal to non-disabled people, and it is discriminatory attitudes and sheer ignorance that prevent disabled people being offered the opportunities given to their non-disabled counterparts.

What is a disability?

There are several ways of defining disability. The most widely used definition is the medical model although disabled people themselves would, as a whole, prefer the social model of disability as this emphasises the social restrictions that prevent disabled people leading fulfilling and rewarding lives. Other lesser known models include the charitable model and the administrative model and due consideration should also be given to these.

The medical model

The most widely used medical definition of disability was composed by the World Health Organisation (WHO) in the early 1980s. This definition defines impairment, disability and handicap as follows:
Impairment – loss or abnormality in structure or function;
Disability – inability to perform an activity within the normal range for a human being, because of an impairment;
Handicap – inability to carry out normal social roles because of an impairment/disability.

These definitions were initially derived for the convenience of medical personnel. They reinforce the misconception that disability is allied to ill health and that disabled people need the care and attention of the medical profession. These definitions also put the responsibility for functional inability with the disabled person and imply that the answers to solving the problems that arise from living with a disability lie with the medical profession.

The social model

The social model looks at the way disabled peoples' lives are affected by the barriers that society imposes. Having a disability certainly implies

that there is some functional limitation that has been caused by an illness, accident or medical condition. In some situations, the limitation is accommodated, i.e. a person with hearing loss may use a hearing aid to restore their hearing; short sightedness can be corrected by wearing glasses or contact lenses. Day-to-day activities may be more difficult for a disabled person because of pain, difficulty in moving or communicating, or because of a learning disability for example, but an understanding and accommodating society would significantly reduce the effects of disability.

If the social and environmental barriers were eliminated, disabled people would be given a more realistic opportunity of living equally alongside non-disabled people.

The charitable model

This model portrays disabled people as needy individuals who rely on the benefaction of others to attain any quality of life. Some disabled people feel that events such as telethons enhance the image of helplessness and dependence, and do nothing to promote equality and independence.

The administrative model

This model is perhaps the least visible because rather than affecting the way disabled people live their immediate lives, it affects the infrastructure of our society. It is derived from an ignorance about the needs of disabled people and other minority groups and consequently their needs are not encompassed as our society is moulded by the higher echelons. The reason why such an ignorance exists is because there are very few disabled people and representatives from other minority groups in powerful decision-making positions.

Types of impairment

The subsequent effects of an illness, accident or medical condition upon the way a person functions can be divided into two main categories: visible and invisible. A visible impairment is one that can be seen, for example a wheelchair user has a very obvious physical impairment. Consequently, may people associate disability with using a wheelchair

when, in fact, wheelchair users make up only a small percentage of the disabled population. There are many other forms of visible and invisible impairments and some examples are listed below. They should not be considered in isolation; a person with advanced diabetes, for example, may have a visual impairment and have mobility difficulties due to slow circulation and loss of sensation.

Physical impairment

This is difficulty in moving or using all or part of the body. The upper limbs may be restricted making it difficult to reach, grasp and manipulate objects; or there may be a mobility impairment often caused by partial or complete loss of function of the legs, but conditions that affect balance or loss of sensation can also result in mobility difficulties. A person with a mobility impairment may not necessarily be dependent on a wheelchair; they may still be ambulant, but find walking difficult.

Sensory impairment

Indicates that there is a loss of hearing or sight.

Learning disability

Suggests that a person has difficulty learning in the commonly used and accepted way, or at the same pace as their peers. It does not mean that they cannot learn; often different approaches to learning will help people with a learning disability to understand.

Communication difficulties

Our main forms of communication are by using speech, gesture and the written word. A communication difficulty may arise when there are difficulties articulating the muscles used for speech or when there are disturbances to the speech area in the brain, for example. We often use

---

If the social and environmental barriers were eliminated, disabled people would be given a more realistic opportunity of living equally alongside non-disabled people

---

gesture to support what we are saying and therefore anyone with a condition that affects their muscle control will have difficulty forming natural gestures.

Mental illness

This includes illnesses that result in disorders of mood, perception, motivation etc., and also conditions that affect the actual brain tissue giving rise to memory loss or disorientation, as found in Alzheimer's disease, for example.

Hidden disability

There are a number of conditions that affect the human body without there being any outward signs of impairment. Conditions such as heart disease, respiratory disorders and epilepsy may affect the person's ability to function effectively in particular situations or at certain times.

Cultural and social influences

What will influence whether and to what extent our lives will be affected by disability? The causes of disability are very diverse and will affect people of all social and cultural backgrounds, but there are some factors that will make us more vulnerable to the causes. For example:

- where we live in the world – e.g. polio and TB are still rife in some developing countries where healthcare provision is inadequate and vaccination programmes have not been fully established;
- income – low income families are more likely to live in homes that are poorly heated, have a less nutritious diet etc., leading to a higher susceptibility to some illnesses;
- lifestyle – the way we live our lives has a direct influence on our health and well-being. Stress, smoking, lack of exercise, recklessness are just a few ways that we put ourselves at risk;
- genetic vulnerability – our body make-up may determine whether we are susceptible to particular illnesses or diseases.

The environment we live in and our financial circumstances will affect how we manage our disability. People who are better off financially are more able to pay for home adaptations and buy in care, should they need it. They have choices that disabled people on low incomes do not have. People who have acquired a disability later in life are more likely to have invested for a secure future. This will in no way alleviate the devastation that disability may cause, but financial security will decrease some of the anxiety about what the future holds. People who are born with a disability may not have had the education and employment opportunities offered to their non-disabled counterparts, and are therefore more likely to be dependent on state benefits and social housing.

Some cultures have a greater commitment to 'family' so that, rightly or wrongly, the immediate and extended family can be relied upon to offer support to the disabled family member. Other cultures have customs that may make life easier or more difficult for disabled people, for example, the way we prepare and eat our food, the clothes we dress in, the way we manage personal tasks etc.

Barriers to ability

Disabled people argue that if attitudes towards them, the way physical environments are designed and the way society is organised were changed, then the effect of their impairments would be minimised, giving them a fairer chance of equality. What can be changed and how?

- The environment – both the internal and external environment can be changed to give better access and improved facilities for disabled people. New public buildings should be designed to meet the requirements of the 'Building Regulations 1991, Approved Document M' which gives guidelines on entrances; internal space, for example doorways and corridors; access to other floors within a building; WC facilities etc. Existing buildings should be adapted wherever possible. Outside, consideration of the needs of disabled people would include, for example, incorporating dropped kerbs at crossings; using

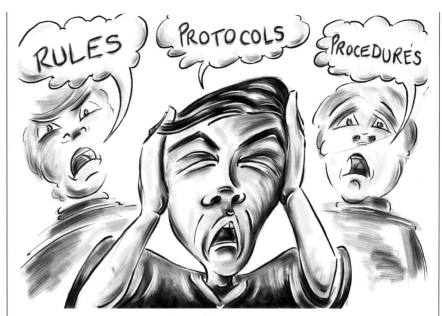

tactile pavement for blind and partially sighted people; locating street furniture in places where it is not going to be an obstruction, and highlighting it by using colour contrast; including parking spaces that are close to amenities and that are wider to allow wheelchair access; providing public toilets that are wheelchair accessible. It is generally thought that good and considerate design is of benefit to all people, not just disabled people.

- The structure of our society – to a certain extent, society dictates to us how we run our lives. We have rules, protocols and procedures that are ensconced in tradition and are very rarely questioned. We conform because we do not want to be different, but sometimes, these traditional values make it difficult for disabled people to 'fit in'. For example, in the work setting, a company may have strict guidelines on how the working week is structured – the day may start at 8.30am with a briefing session, making it difficult for a disabled person who needs extra time in the morning to get dressed and to the office, to attend. But, if the employer introduced flexitime and scheduled meetings for the middle of the working day, the disabled person would not have any difficulty attending.

- Access to information – we rely on written material for academic studies, and in our day-to-day lives for example, to tell us what time the buses are running and how our kitchen appliances operate. This information is only useful to people who can read and understand what they are reading. To help people with disabilities, information should be available in plain English, large print, spoken (on audio cassette or via a speech synthesiser) and Braille. People who are unable to hear the spoken word should have access to a sign language interpreter, or subtitles if the information is on screen.

- Attitudinal barriers – many people have preconceived ideas about what disabled people are like, and fears probably because they have had little contact with disabled people in the past. This can lead to patronising attitudes, or intolerance because they have not recognised that a disabled person may (through no fault of their own) take longer to do something or tire more easily. People may automatically adopt a discriminatory attitude by making an incorrect assumption that a disabled person would not be as capable as a non-disabled person.

• The above information is an extract from a factsheet entitled *Disability awareness* produced by the Disabled Living Foundation (DLF). See their web site at www.dlf.org.uk or see their address details on page 41.

Disabled customers

Mystery shoppers show up the gaps in provision for disabled customers. Information from the Employers' Forum on Disability

Many shops and businesses in the UK need to improve their services for disabled people if they are to comply with Part III of the DDA, according to a new survey carried out by management services company and Forum member the Grass Roots Group.

The research reveals that, although real progress has been made, major deficiencies still exist in the standard of service disabled people receive.

The research targeted 50 of the UK's largest companies to gain the most optimistic picture of the level of service currently provided for disabled people.

The study was undertaken by a team of mystery shoppers, drawn from a panel of 2,000 disabled people across the UK, who visited the premises of 289 building societies, high street shops, supermarkets and telephone call centres.

The team included blind and partially sighted people, wheelchair users, deaf and hard of hearing people and people with mobility problems, facial disfigurements and speech impediments.

A group of non-disabled shoppers was used to compare the standard of service they received with that received by their disabled counterparts.

The findings showed that four out of five companies visited were not able to provide standard information in alternative formats such as Braille or audiotape. Forty per cent of wheelchair users had difficulties entering premises, and almost half (44%) of those with mobility problems found counter heights to be a problem.

> *Although real progress has been made, major deficiencies still exist in the standard of service disabled people receive*

Forty-three per cent of mobility-impaired customers could not reach leaflets easily, and over half (57%) of the disabled people who required staff assistance were not given the help they needed. Seventy per cent of profoundly deaf people found that customer service staff were not able to meet their particular needs.

Although eight out of 10 disabled researchers perceived staff to be confident in dealing with their needs, 54% felt staff had not received disability training. There was often a welcome desire to help, but an acute lack of knowledge of how to go about it. The research showed progress on the accessibility of exits and entrances in high street retailers, banks and building societies, though food retailers performed less well. Financial institutions scored highest for providing aids for hard of hearing people (such as induction loop systems), although less than a third provided them and half of those provided did not work.

Grass Roots chairman and chief executive David Evans said: 'Our report is "encouraging but room for improvement". Part III of the DDA is nearly upon us and it is evident that even the leading shops and businesses need to improve their act.'

For more information, contact Stephen Lloyd at the Grass Roots Group on 01442 829 400.

• The above information is from the Employers' Forum on Disability's web site which can be found at www.employers-forum.co.uk

© *The Employers' Forum on Disability*

Poverty and benefits

Information from Disability Daily

Low incomes, high costs

There are over 8.6 million disabled people in the UK,[1] most of whom live in, or on the edge of, poverty. Disabled people face a combination of lower incomes and higher expenses. Day-to-day living brings extra costs directly related to impairment – such as extra heating or laundry, particular dietary needs, additional wear and tear on clothing or household items, communication equipment, accessible travel, paying for cleaning, shopping, personal care and medicines.

The majority of disabled people rely on social security benefits as a main source of income and therefore the level at which benefits are paid is vital in preventing poverty and enabling people to live full and independent lives.

Disability living allowance (DLA) has been very successful in providing over 2 million disabled people with help towards their extra costs. However, age discrimination means that the vast majority of older disabled people get less benefit, since they can only claim the more limited attendance allowance (AA). In addition, Government research has estimated that up to 60 per cent of people eligible for DLA fail to claim it.

Incapacity benefit, intended to replace earnings for those unable to work because of ill-health or disability, is worth less than 17% of average earnings and is means-tested from April 2001 for those with their own pensions.

Despite facing extra heating costs, disabled people under 60 do not receive the winter fuel payment worth £200, which all pensioners now get.

The Government recently increased the savings threshold for people over 60 who are on means-tested benefits. Yet disabled people under 60 start to lose benefit if they have over £3,000 in savings – making it virtually impossible to save for large

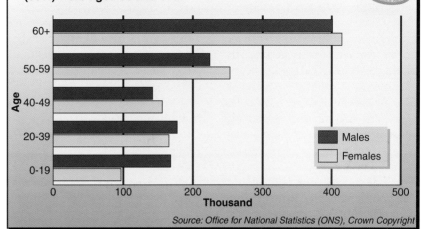

Disability Living Allowance

- **The number of people receiving disability living allowance increased by 5% in the year ending 30 November 2000 to 2.2 million.**
- **Of these people, 579 thousand received only the mobility component, 297 thousand received only the care component and 1.32 million received both mobility and care components.**
- **Just over half (51%) of the total recipients were males and over half (59%) were aged 50 and over.**

Source: Office for National Statistics (ONS), Crown Copyright

items of equipment like an electric wheelchair.

The introduction of the disabled persons' tax credit in October 1999 for working disabled people on low wages was very welcome. However, eligibility for the tax credit is more restrictive than the working families' tax credit. Because it is means-tested, disabled people with a working partner lose out and those on housing benefit see very little improvement in their overall income. In addition, the credit is only available to those working longer than 16 hours a week – too much for many disabled people who would nevertheless like to do some work.

Recommendations

The new Government should:
- Make lifting disabled people out of poverty a priority for the Social Exclusion Unit and create a similar target to that set for reducing child poverty.
- Work with local authorities and voluntary organisations to increase take-up of DLA and AA.
- End age discrimination within DLA, so that people who become

disabled over the age of 65 can still claim.
- Extend the winter fuel payment to disabled people getting disability living allowance.
- Increase incapacity benefit to a realistic level and then annually in line with earnings.
- Increase the savings limit for means-tested benefits so that it is the same for disabled people whatever their age.
- Amend the disabled persons' tax credit so that it is linked to earnings but not subject to a household means-test. Change eligibility rules so that anyone who is disabled and on a low wage can qualify. Abolish the 16 hours rule.

Reference
1. 'Disability in Great Britain' DSS research report 94 July 99.

• The above information is from *The Disability Manifesto – for rights, equality and inclusion* produced by Disability Daily, a consortium of agencies and carers.

© *Disability Daily*

Benefits for the extra costs of disability

Information from the National Association of Citizens' Advice Bureaux

There are two benefits which are payable to a person to help with the extra costs of disability. These are:

- disability living allowance – see below; or
- attendance allowance – see below.

A person who is getting disability living allowance or attendance allowance may also be able to claim benefits for not being able to work because s/he is sick or income related benefits. However, disability living allowance and attendance allowance can be paid to a person who works and are not affected by any work a person does. Disability living allowance and attendance allowance are disregarded as income for income-related benefits. They can be paid in addition to any other income.

Disability living allowance

Disability living allowance can be paid to a person with a disability who:

- claims before s/he is 65 and her/his care or mobility needs began before s/he was 65; and
- is not permanently in hospital or living in accommodation provided by or funded by a local authority; and
- has lived in the UK for six out of the last 12 months and actually lives in the UK when s/he claims and normally lives in the UK, unless s/he is terminally ill; and
- has care needs – see below; and/or
- has mobility needs – see below.

Care needs

A person will have care needs if s/he:

- needs help with 'bodily functions', for example, eating, washing, dressing and going to the toilet. It can also include help which enables someone to take part in social activities; and/or
- needs supervision to stop being a danger to her/himself or others; and/or
- needs help in preparing and cooking a main meal, for example, s/he cannot cope with heavy pans or cannot light a cooker; and/or
- is terminally ill.

It does not matter if no one is providing the person with care, but s/he must show that s/he needs the care.

Mobility needs

A person will have mobility needs if s/he:

- cannot walk outdoors or go on an unfamiliar route without guidance or supervision from another person most of the time, for example, s/he is blind; or
- is unable to walk or has difficulty in walking. This may mean using a wheelchair, walking very slowly, walking with a lot of pain or effort or being unable to walk very far; or
- has had both legs amputated or was born without legs or feet; or
- is blind and deaf and needs someone to help her/him out of doors; or
- has severe learning difficulties and can behave very disruptively.

It does not matter if no one is providing the claimant with the guidance or supervision s/he needs.

How much will the claimant get?

There are two components of disability living allowance. The care component is for care needs and the mobility component is for mobility needs. The claimant can receive one or both components.

The care component is paid at three rates:

- the lower rate is paid for somebody who needs help with cooking a main meal or who needs care for a significant part of the day
- the middle rate is paid to someone who needs frequent care throughout the day or during the night
- the higher rate is paid to someone who needs frequent care throughout the day and during the night, or who is terminally ill.

The mobility component is paid at two rates:

- the lower rate is paid to someone who cannot walk outdoors without guidance or supervision
- the higher rate is paid to anyone else.

Disability living allowance
Weekly rate (From 12.4.01)

Care component

High	£55.30
Middle	£37.00
Low	£14.65

Mobility component

High	£38.65
Lower	£14.65

Disability living allowance will be paid as long as the person has care/mobility needs and may be awarded for an indefinite period or a fixed period. It cannot be paid until the person has had care/mobility needs for three months and the needs must be expected to last for at least six months. The time limits do not apply if the person is terminally ill and claims the care component. Disability living allowance is affected by going into hospital. Disability living allowance will usually stop after four weeks in hospital (twelve weeks if the person is under 16).

How to claim disability living allowance

A person can claim disability living allowance by:

- telephoning the Benefits Enquiry Line (BEL)
- obtaining a claim pack by completing leaflet DS704, available from post offices and social security offices. Some organisations are also authorised to hold claim packs, for example, Citizens' Advice Bureaux.

The claimant will need a health professional to complete part of the form.

The claimant must provide her/his national insurance (NI) number or information which will enable it to be identified. If s/he does not have a NI number, s/he should apply for one.

After the Benefits Agency receive the form, the claimant may have to have a medical examination.

Attendance allowance

Attendance allowance can be paid to a person with a disability who:

- is aged over 66 or between 65 and 66 and her/his disability began on or after her/his 65th birthday; and
- is not permanently in hospital or living in accommodation provided by or funded by a local authority; and
- has lived in the UK for 6 out of the last 12 months, actually lives in the UK when s/he claims and normally lives in the UK, unless s/he is terminally ill; and
- has care needs – see below.

Care needs

A person will have care needs if s/he:

- needs help with 'bodily functions', for example, washing, dressing and going to the toilet. It can also include help which enables someone to take part in social activities; and/or

- needs supervision to stop her/himself being in danger to her/himself or others; and/or
- is terminally ill.

It does not matter if no one is providing the person with care, but s/he must show that s/he needs the care.

How much will the claimant get?

Attendance allowance is paid at two rates:

- the lower rate is paid to somebody who needs frequent care throughout the day or night. From 9 April 2001, the lower rate is £37.00
- the higher rate is paid to someone who needs frequent care throughout the day and the night, or who is terminally ill. From 9 April 2001, the higher rate is £55.30

Attendance allowance will be paid as long as the person has care needs and may be awarded for a fixed or indefinite period. It cannot be paid until the person has had care needs for six months. This time limit does not apply if the person is terminally ill. Attendance allowance will stop after four weeks in hospital.

How to claim attendance allowance

A person can claim attendance allowance by:

- telephoning the Benefits Enquiry Line (BEL)
- obtaining a claim pack by completing leaflet DS704, available from post offices and social security offices. Some organisations are also authorised to hold packs, for example, Citizens' Advice Bureaux.

The claimant will need a health professional to complete part of the form.

The claimant must provide her/his national insurance number or information which will enable it to be identified. If s/he does not have a number, s/he should apply for one.

After the Benefits Agency receive the form, the claimant may have to have a medical examination.

• This information is an extract from the National Association of Citizens' Advice Bureaux's web site which can be found at www.nacab.org.uk Information is checked and updated regularly. This information incorporates changes made up to 9 May 2001. Check their web site for the latest data.

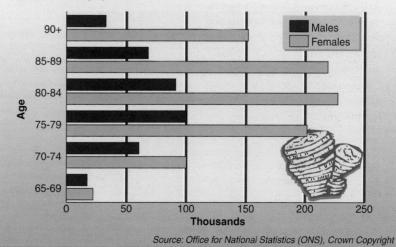

Attendance allowance

- **The number of people receiving attendance allowance increased by 2.7% in the year ending 30 November 2000 to 1.29 million.**

- **The majority (71%) of these were females and over a half (61%) of all people were aged 80 and over.**

- **The main cause of disability was arthritis (378 thousand) representing 29% of all causes.**

- **The proportion of people receiving AA by region varied from 16 per 1,000 head of population in London and the South East to 32 per 1,000 head of population in Wales.**

Source: Office for National Statistics (ONS), Crown Copyright

Disabled children

Child poverty is a disability issue

The Government has committed itself to an ambitious target of ending child poverty within 20 years. Among the children most likely to be living in poverty are the 360,000 disabled children in the UK. Recent increases in benefits for disabled children have been an important step in tackling poverty among this group. However, there is more to be done.

Choices and rights

There is an urgent need to ensure that disabled children can enjoy the same rights as their peers. Disabled children can find it doubly hard to get their voices heard, with non-disabled adults making most of the decisions affecting their lives. Policy makers and practitioners should listen to disabled children and take them into account.

Recommendations

The new Government should:
- Ensure that the UN Convention on the Rights of the Child is implemented fully in all areas of Government policy and legislation affecting disabled children
- Establish a Commissioner for Children and Young People in England, Wales, Scotland and Northern Ireland.
- Ensure that families with disabled children are made aware of the social security benefits to which they may be entitled. Families of all children with a statement of special educational needs should automatically be given information about disability living allowance, and any other benefits for which they might qualify.
- Provide more resources to promote the inclusion of disabled children and young people in all education and leisure facilities, for example by providing extra learning support assistants in schools.
- Ensure that disability equality, the identification of special educational need, and classroom strategies to overcome any obstacles these present, are an integral part of initial teacher training.
- Ring-fence Standard Fund monies for LEAs and schools to purchase disability awareness training for staff ('inset days') according to the profile of SEN in the area or school.
- School league tables should include indicators of the inclusion of, and educational outcomes for, both disabled children and those with special educational needs. Support for disabled children and those with SEN are good indicators of a supportive school culture.
- Use the new 'Connexions' strategy to support disabled young people to realise their aspirations. Transition planning for disabled school leavers should include a full benefits-check and bring together education, health, career, housing and social services to plan coherently for the future.

• The above information is from *The Disability Manifesto – for rights, equality and inclusion* produced by Disability Daily, a consortium of agencies and carers.

© *Disability Daily*

Disability in the UK

Some facts and figures

- there are approximately 8.7 million disabled people in the UK covered by the Disability Discrimination Act, which represents around 15 per cent of the population
- some 70 per cent of economically active disabled people became disabled during their working lives
- over 5.2 million disabled people are of working age which represents 18 per cent of the working population
- however, only 42 per cent of disabled people of working age are in employment compared to 81 per cent of non-disabled people of working age
- disabled people are over six times as likely as non-disabled people to be out of work and claiming benefits. Of the 2.4 million disabled people on state benefits and not in work nearly a million would like to work
- fewer than 5 per cent of disabled people use wheelchairs
- by the year 2010, 40 per cent of the UK population will be over 45 – the age at which the incidence of disability begins to increase significantly
- one in every four customers either has a disability or has a close relative or friend who is disabled
- the estimated annual purchasing power of people with disabilities is £40-£50 billion.

  Statistics from the ONS, NCSR, RADAR, EFD

• The above information is from the Employers' Forum on Disability's web site which can be found at www.employers-forum.co.uk

© *The Employers' Forum on Disability*

Talking my language

Clare Evans, Manager of the Leonard Cheshire Disabled People's Forum, addresses the fundamental importance of using the right language

'Disabled people' not 'cripples' or 'handicapped'. 'Wheelchair users' not 'wheelchair bound'. Is it important what language we use in everyday conversation? Is there an underlying reason as to why people should use appropriate language? And, how do they know what is appropriate?

Yes – it is important because language is the way we communicate with each other as human beings and thus reflects our thoughts and attitudes from within. Often, non-disabled people's low expectations and stereotypical views about disabled people are reflected in the way they refer to or speak about them rather than just in the language they use.

As a senior member of staff at Leonard Cheshire and Manager of the Disabled People's Forum, I frequently visit residential homes for meetings with other managers. Staff or volunteers associated with the home fail to ask my identity, instead making automatic assumptions because I'm a disabled person. It is more usual, on these occasions, for people not to see me as a potential member of staff, because I am a wheelchair user – people notice the wheelchair beyond all other means of identification. On my latest visit, when my partner was acting as a care assistant, a volunteer said to him (not me of course!) 'when is your wife thinking of moving in?'

The language people use often shows the inappropriate attitudes they have towards disabled people. Some commonly used terms reflect an attitude of the tragedy of being disabled, often associated historically with charities. In this, disabled people are referred to as heroic because their impairments cause them suffering. This is essentially negative and limiting, because it suggests that disabled people are weaker, more dependent and less able than non-disabled people. This attitude

Creating opportunities with disabled people

LEONARD CHESHIRE

undermines and distances disabled people from the rest of society.

Often the comments made reflect assumptions people have about disabled people playing a different role in society. They are not, for instance, expected to be in gainful employment, paying taxes and contributing to society's well-being. People therefore have difficulty dealing with disabled people who do work. A taxi driver who recently took me to work referred to my employment patronisingly as 'it's nice that you're keeping yourself busy'. They are unable to equate a disabled person's work as a contribution to society and view it only as therapy for the disabled person.

The way disabled people are referred to reflects deeply held assumptions about how they differ from 'normal' members of society. It was noticeable, for example, when my impairment increased and I started to use a wheelchair more frequently, that strangers would refer to me – a wife and mother – as 'Miss'

and assume I was single. The language people often use not only de-sexes disabled people but shows that they think disabled people don't have relationships and get married.

References to disabled people can show the prejudices of the caring profession. For example, managers may refer to 'bed spaces' when meaning the occupancy rates of residents' rooms. And those with high support needs are frequently referred to in professional shorthand as the 'heavy end' of caring – these terms dehumanise us. We are reduced to being seen as passive and dependent when staff talk about feeding us instead of assisting us to eat and toileting us instead of assisting us to use the toilet ourselves.

Knowing what's appropriate.

Language is a moveable feast because it evolves as society changes, which makes an added difficulty since it changes the way in which people want to be referred to. It used to be most appropriate to refer to disabled people as 'people with disabilities'. The thinking behind this was that people were seen as people first and their disabilities only came afterwards.

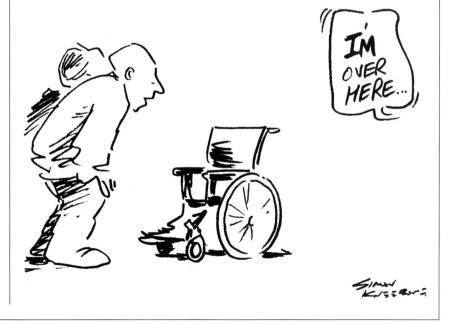

However, with the development of the social model of disability within the disabled people's movement, it has been recognised that it is the attitudes and environments within society that exclude disabled people from full participation rather than the problem being within the person. This means that other people's low expectations disable them, that the inaccessibility of a bus disables them, not the fact that they have impaired vision or cerebral palsy. So now it is more appropriate to use the term disabled people, referring to the reason why society disables people because of a physical, sensory or intellectual impairment they may have.

So language, which reflects attitudes, is significant in the way it can disempower disabled people if used inappropriately. Disabled people, constantly facing prejudice through the language people use, are inevitably affected by it. Negative, patronising, passive language causes low self-esteem and low sense of self-worth. It is difficult for disabled people not to take on the assumptions of society at large and to continually find the energy to keep challenging such attitudes. It's worth trying to get it right, isn't it?

Media disability

Every day newspapers keep around 14 million people informed and entertained, offering analysis and opinion on the day's key issues. With this measure of power and influence it is essential that journalists get it right when they write about disabled people. But, a recent report by Scope, a national disability organisation whose focus is on people with cerebral palsy, has proved that they don't.

After analysing national papers for eight weeks and local papers for four weeks, Scope found that: 'stories relating to disabled people concentrate most on medical research, medical negligence and court cases. In local papers, fund-raising initiatives by or for disabled people were the most popular. Story selection was not the only problem. Disabled people are still commonly described using outdated stereotypes and pejorative terms.'*

It is vital that journalists become responsible for the power they have in influencing society's attitudes towards disabled people and become sensitive to the way that their words perpetuate discrimination. As Clare Evans, Manager of the Leonard Cheshire Disabled People's Forum, says: 'Sometimes, if people are unaware of the sensitivities around language, they can unintentionally cause offence. In a citation for a national award, for example, a colleague of mine nominated a disabled person as a "wheelchair user with arthritis". The people promoting the awards, however, were unaware of the sensitivities of using the correct language and so this was changed in the national press to "wheelchair bound arthritis sufferer".'

As long as newspapers continue to propagate negative views of disability, the negative effect this has on disabled people and non-disabled people's perceptions of them is obvious.

Not only this, journalists should wake up to the fact that one in four of their readers are disabled people.

Stop Press! How the press portrays disabled people, Campaigns Department, Scope 2000.

• The above information is reproduced from *Compass*, Leonard Cheshire's international magazine. See page 41 for address details.

© *Leonard Cheshire, 2001*

A role for the disabled

The advertising industry regularly comes under attack from pressure groups for the people in ads: not enough black people, not enough Asians, not enough fat people, not enough disabled. The industry shuffles its feet and promises to do better – and gradually things change.

Two years ago, after the Glenn Hoddle furore, the Leonard Cheshire Foundation started a campaign to increase the number of disabled people in ads. Last week, the message finally got through to the Government. As the country's largest advertiser, spending more than £100m a year, it has promised, where possible, to feature more disabled people.

There are, however, fears that agencies may be forced to toe the line of political correctness. Clearly, some government ads – for the Army or nurses, for example – would not make much sense with disabled people. There's no reason, however, why ads about education, the New Deal, tax credits and drink driving couldn't accommodate the disabled.

Commercial ads already feature disabled people quite prominently. Coca-Cola and Sauza tequila featured blind people and Sony PlayStation a black man in a wheelchair. Stephen Hawking has appeared for both BT and Specsavers; Freeserve has Aimee Mullins, a disabled model; and Fuji has used people with Down's Syndrome.

It shows that if advertisers put their minds to it, it's really quite easy to do.

© *Telegraph Group Limited, London 2000*

Human wrongs

The rights of disabled people are being ignored by the UN

By Raekha Prasad

There are more than 500 UN conventions, including many designed to protect groups deemed to be at risk, such as children, women, and refugees. But despite a campaign launched in the 1980s, there is still no convention on the rights of people with disabilities.

An estimated 600m people worldwide have a disability, eight in 10 of whom are in developing countries. Of them, 82% live below the poverty line. For campaigners demanding a convention, disability seems to be the final frontier of equality.

The profile of the campaign will be boosted tomorrow by a conference in London of global disability activists. The event has been organised by International Service (IS), a York-based agency, which says it sees disabled people routinely excluded from mainstream development processes in the countries where it sends volunteers. Representatives of disability groups in Africa, Palestine and Latin America are being flown to London by IS to discuss how to build coalitions and enlist the support of governments, including Britain's.

Campaigners believe that discrimination against disabled people, and breaches of their human rights, are issues not adequately addressed by the UN standard rules on equalisation of opportunities for those with disabilities. These rules state what governments 'should' do to ensure that disabled people can participate equally in all areas of life, including education, medical care, employment and the family. But activists argue that the rules lack clout because they are not legally binding.

By contrast, member states have to report to the UN on the progress they make on ratified conventions. This enables civil rights organisations to monitor their government's actions and demand accountability. As UN human rights committees do not currently deal with disability abuses, documenting the level and nature of such abuse is difficult. This gap has prompted a British organisation, Disability Awareness in Action (DAA), to invite disabled people to send in testimonies for a human rights database. It has recorded abuses affecting more than 2m disabled people and claims that almost a quarter of victims have endured a breach of article three of the UN declaration of human rights, which states that 'everyone has the right to life, liberty and security of person'. In addition, more than a fifth had been subjected to 'torture or . . . cruel, inhuman or degrading treatment or punishment' in breach of article five of the declaration.

Richard Light, DAA's research director, says: 'Existing rules have failed to prevent prejudiced attitudes. Doctors, for example, are still withholding treatment from disabled people because the underlying attitude is "better dead than disabled". Even among many human rights monitoring organisations, abuses in mental health institutions, such as the use of ECT [electro-convulsive therapy] without consent, are seen as medical issues and not to do with human rights.'

Light acknowledges that a convention has limitations – there is no international court to enforce it –

An estimated 600m people worldwide have a disability, eight in 10 of whom are in developing countries. Of them, 82% live below the poverty line

but says it would be 'an official and formal recognition that disabled people are human beings'.

The path to a UN convention, as past campaigns prove, is long and arduous. Jane Carter, chief executive of IS, points out that the drive for a convention on the rights of the child lasted more than 60 years. 'We hope it doesn't take that long,' she says of the goal of a disability convention, 'but it has got to be raised again and again.'

Richard Howitt, a Labour MEP and president of the EU all-party disability intergroup, suggests that the campaign is hampered by a perception of disability rights as non-political and therefore uncontroversial. 'It's been seen as a charity issue, which means it's not a priority,' he says. 'It's been treated in a patronising and paternalistic way.'

Howitt, who will address the conference, says it was a major breakthrough when the EU agreed to include action against disability discrimination in the 1997 Amsterdam treaty. 'All the wise owls of Europe said: "You'll never include disability" – and we did. It was all down to clever lobbying and political campaigning.'

But, he adds, the EU does not extend disability rights into policy-making. 'If we had a convention, it would have to inform thinking in areas such as justice, asylum and foreign affairs.'

Member states are 'very nervous' about a UN convention, Howitt admits. But he is optimistic that it will come. 'It's a matter of time, rather than if it will happen.'

Ireland has taken a pro-convention lead within the UN. Eamonn MacAodha, first secretary at the Irish mission to the UN and also a speaker at the conference, says: 'The issue is so important, it does merit a separate convention. But while countries such as South Africa support it, relatively few western nations do.'

Disability discrimination

Information from the Industrial Society

Definition

Under the Disability Discrimination Act 1995 (DDA), the Government defines disability as: 'A physical or mental impairment which has a substantial and long-term effect on a person's ability to carry out normal day-to-day activities.'

- Impairment covers physical or mobility impairments, sensory impairment, learning disabilities and mental health needs. Long-term means likely to last 12 months or more, or likely to recur.
- The Act also covers severe dis-figurements and progressive symptomatic conditions, where impairments are likely to become substantial. It excludes alcoholics and those with certain personality disorders.

Background

Placement, Assessment and Counselling Teams (PACTs) were set up in April 1992 to work with employers and disabled people. The aim is to offer support to those in, or looking for, work.

- Access to Work (ATW) is a programme organised by PACTs to give employers financial help for employment support services to help a disabled person work. Employers pay 20% of the cost of equipment and ATW provides the rest.
- The National Disability Council (NDC) and the Northern Ireland Disability Council (NIDC) were set up to advise the Government on reducing discrimination and implementing the Act.
- People with disabilities now have statutory rights to non-discrimination in employment and access to goods and services, as well as other rights, not directly linked to employment. The measures on employment came into force in December 1996.
- Less favourable treatment can be justified if the treatment is relevant to the circumstances of the individual case, or if the reason is substantial and cannot be reasonably overcome or reduced.
- Employers are required to make reasonable adjustments to their employment arrangements or premises if they substantially disadvantage disabled applicants or employees. This includes reasonable changes to premises, fixtures and fittings, furniture and stairways.
- All employees in organisations of 20 or more employees are covered, including part-timers, temporary staff and those on contract.

Key facts

- 56 cases have been heard under the DDA and six have been successful. Some failed because the discrimination took place before the Act came into force, and some because the employer

---

1.7 million people are, at any one time, temporarily disabled through injury or old age

---

was not fully aware of the disability. In October 1997, 16 cases were adjourned.

- Several hundred more are waiting to be heard or settled before going to tribunal. An unknown number have been settled after initial complaints.
- The Government is setting up a Disability Rights Commission to protect, enforce and promote disabled people's rights under the Act. The Minister for Equal Opportunities and Employment recognised that the lack of an enforcing body had been a fundamental flaw in the Act. The Commission will bring disability discrimination in line with that for race and sex, and should replace the disability councils (the NDC and the NIDC).
- Welfare to Work measures should benefit disabled people. £195 million will be allocated for specific measures aimed at the disabled, whether or not they have been unemployed for six months.
- There are currently 3.9 million disabled people of working age, but under a third of them are employed.
- 1.7 million people are, at any one

time, temporarily disabled through injury or old age.

- Two codes of practice have been published, one on employment, the other on rights of access to goods, facilities, services and premises. They have no legal force, but may be taken into account by tribunals and courts.
- About half the respondents to an Employment Trends survey in September 1996 have used PACTs, either to help with broad policies, or an individual employee with a disability. Just over a third of survey respondents had used ATW.
- A RADAR survey on the scheme found it generally effective, but it recommended increasing funding.
- A survey of over 200 employers in January 1997 (IRS Equal Opportunities Report) found that:
  – 96% had allocated responsibility for complying with the DDA;
  – 87% had a written policy on employing the disabled, and 10% planned one;
  – 31% had made changes and 17% planned changes to policy in preparing for the DDA;
  – two-thirds had given training for HR managers on the Act, only 28% had done so for line managers; and
  – less than a quarter believe the law will make a significant change.

State of play

The number of cases brought so far is much less than expected. The reasons for this include:

– legal aid is not available; and

– many people with disabilities may not know the full provisions of the law.

It may be that some cases are being taken under civil law to the Crown Court, but there are no central statistics on this.

The reasons so few cases have been successful are also complex:

– tribunals are still setting their own benchmarks; and

– some seem confused about which disabilities are covered. Many cases concerning multiple

sclerosis were not covered at first and were rejected, but now it is covered by the Act.

Best practice guidelines

- Policy on disability discrimination needs to be part of the organisation's overall diversity or equal opportunities policy, demonstrating that the organisation values contributions from all sections of the community.
- Draft, display and circulate your organisation's statement of commitment to fair employment practice, access and training.
- Ensure employees and contractors know what constitutes discrimination and provide disability awareness training, particularly for those recruiting employees.
- Regularly review employment practices and customer service arrangements to ensure compliance with the law.
- Conduct an access audit and form an action plan with deadlines for implementation and review.
- Set up a consultation group to co-ordinate feedback and action, and an effective complaints procedure to handle feedback.
- Work with local and national organisations to gain information.
- Monitor and publicise good results.

• The above information is an extract from the Industrial Society's series of Management Factsheets. See page 41 for their address details.

Regional disabled people still excluded from work

Disabled people in the south are still being excluded from jobs according to a survey of managers in the region conducted by Leonard Cheshire, the UK's largest disability care charity.

Despite an improvement in management attitudes towards disability, with 100% regarding disabled people as an asset to an organisation, 92% of respondents do not work directly with a disabled person and 97% employed fewer disabled people than the national average of 2%.

The survey was conducted amongst 140 local employers and managers who attended an event at Microsoft's Campus at Thames Valley Park where they heard about the opportunities and obligations of the Disability Discrimination Act and Leonard Cheshire's IT training and employment programme Workability.

John Knight, head of external policy at Leonard Cheshire, said: 'The findings show that there is still a long way to go in improving job opportunities for disabled people. Only once disabled people are able to work and make their own living will we start to achieve social inclusion.'

One barrier identified as an obstacle to recruiting and retaining disabled staff was the belief that making adjustments to equipment and premises is prohibitively expensive.

Mike Gomm, Centre Manager for AbilityNet in Reading, an organisation specialising in working with disabled people and employers to find solutions to IT problems based on the Microsoft campus, said: 'This is a total misconception of the situation. In many cases adaptions to technology can cost as little as £50 and in some cases they can be free – it's often just about knowing how to use existing technology and much of Microsoft's software already contains applications that help.'

• Reproduced from Leonard Cheshire's web site www.leonard-cheshire.org

Call to give disabled real job opportunities

A change of strategy within the government means councils are dropping schemes to create jobs for people with disabilities. That's OK say campaigners, as long as employers accommodate people of all abilities

By Alex Dobson

Paternalistic work environments should be consigned to history, according to disability rights campaigners.

In tune with the times, the government has been responding with new measures aimed at putting disabled workers alongside other able-bodied workers in the community. But there are fears that these may mean that some disabled people employed by local authorities will be in danger of losing their jobs. Under new regulations, councils are no longer required to help fund sheltered workplaces.

From this month on, individual authorities are no longer required to pay 25% towards the cost of sheltered workplaces. At a time when many local authority social services departments are under pressure to make savings to deal with overspends, there are growing concerns that one casualty may be the jobs that are currently offered to disabled workers.

At Gloucestershire county council, the social services department needs to make savings of £6.5m out of a budget of £88.5m. One option is to make around 50 disabled people, who are employed at the council's industrial units, redundant. The units, Gloucester Industrial Services (GIS), employ more than 200 people working on reconditioning wheelchairs and making double-glazed windows.

'The government is not placing the same conditions on us to joint-fund sheltered workshops as it did in the past,' says Mark Branton, assistant director of social services.

'It is placing targets on us that are about moving disabled people into real employment in the private sector, as opposed to real employment within the units. The impact of that is that there isn't the same requirement for us to be providing subsidised employment.'

And, he points out: 'That means that we have to consider whether we should keep a sheltered industrial unit, when most of the government's strategy, in terms of the welfare to work programme, is finding work for disabled people in the community. It is not about running sheltered workshops ourselves, and many local authorities no longer run them at all. It is about using that resource occasionally as a way of providing rehabilitation to people.'

> **'At present, not all employers are geared to providing the level of support that some disabled workers need'**

Although major providers of employment for disabled people – including Remploy, which currently has over 10,000 disabled employees – agree that the aim should be to see as many disabled people as possible working in the community, they stress that what is needed is more options.

'Although the long-term aim should be to get as many disabled people into the community as possible, there is a need for a range of employment, because we have to recognise that the needs of disabled people are different. At present, not all employers are geared to providing the level of support that some disabled workers need,' says Ray Fletcher, director of personnel at Remploy.

The charities Scope and Mencap also emphasise that, while supporting disabled people's right to acceptance in the workplace is vital, flexibility in what is offered is just as important.

Mike Stubley has first-hand knowledge of working in a sheltered workplace. He works at GIS as a production superintendent and is disabled himself.

He agrees that the broad intention behind the government's strategy for the disabled is correct but argues that the reality for many disabled people is that the kind of sheltered workplace offered at GIS is likely to prove most successful for some disabled people.

'Unfortunately, not everyone is capable of working in open employment. The experience of many of us who work in sheltered employment with disabled people with different levels of disability is that we know that, for many, especially some of the older people, a sheltered workplace is a good environment for them to work in. It is important to see people as individuals and cater for them appropriately. In an ideal world, there would be adequate support and flexibility in all open employment – but this is not an ideal world,' he said.

Sarah Everett, branch secretary of public sector union Unison in Gloucester, said the union would fight any attempt at making workers at GIS redundant and that one way of doing so may be to invoke the new human rights legislation. A decision from the local authority is expected next month.

Disability does not mean inability

The Civil Service is one employer widening graduate recruitment

By Emma Williams

Disabled people in the UK are six times more likely to be unemployed than non-disabled people, government research has found. And contrary to popular opinion, the term 'disability' no longer only refers to those bound to wheelchairs. It can include those who are hard of hearing, visually impaired or suffering from depression. Even when disabled people are in employment, the research shows they tend to remain in low status jobs. 'The figures are horrendous. Work is a civil right,' Margaret Hodge, the Minister for Disabled People, recently admitted.

The Civil Service is one organisation at the forefront of doing something about it. 'Diversity is our current focus, particularly when it comes to graduate recruitment,' says spokesman Simon Fryer, who points to the recently developed Diversity Division which, apart from aiming to recruit more staff who are female and from ethnic minorities, has set itself a target of doubling the number of disabled staff in senior positions by 2005. Fryer is quick to add that since 70 per cent of disabled workers become disabled during their working lives, 'our focus isn't exclusively on recruiting people who are already disabled. It's about letting recruits know that if this is something that happens to them later on, they don't need to worry about facing discrimination.'

Susan Scott-Parker, chief executive of the Employers' Forum on Disability, believes the Civil Service's aims should appeal to all graduates, irrespective of whether they are disabled. 'An employer who focuses on disability is an employer who is likely to be fair in other areas and who has an eye for good business sense,' she says. 'Disabled staff tend to stay longer with a business, which reduces training costs, and they take less time off sick. Dealing with a disability makes people good problem solvers.'

After graduating in 1997, Vicky Waite, 30, spent a year on incapacity benefits. Now part of the financial systems team in the Cabinet Office, she says her job has turned her life around. 'The civil service immediately recognised that my disability did not affect my performance.' Waite first entered the Civil Service on a work experience placement through the charity 'Workable', which specialises in placing disabled graduates. She is provided with subsidised transport and a specially adjusted work-station 'but more important is their willingness to understand and allow me to take breaks when needed'. In fact, the Cabinet Office even provide a bed for her in a private room.

As a result of the range of initiatives developed by the Civil Service, there has been a rise in the number of disabled applicants, says Fryer. 'Among these initiatives are the rules that applicants who meet the minimum criteria must be interviewed; there must be regular consultation and progress reviews;

there is a commitment to improving knowledge awareness; and if staff become disabled during their employment, we make every effort to retain them.'

Nevertheless, argues Jennifer Knight, equal opportunities officer from the Department of Education and Employment, work still needs to be done. 'Staff need to be more aware of the service's willingness to make the working environment more accessible to them.' Workshops, she says, are proving particularly effective in facing such challenges. 'We have run several, which address how to make the application process easier through reaching specific audiences and working with other agencies.'

According to Sue Ward, who studies disability issues in the Cabinet Office, one of the main problems in both attracting and retaining disabled staff is that people find it hard to volunteer information about their situation.

'If you don't put your hand up, you can't find out what help is available,' agrees Simon Winkler, a business manager in the Cabinet Office. A heart transplant left him in need of special working arrangements seven years ago. 'I can't fault my employers,' he says. 'They have allowed me to work flexibly from home two days a week and they provided all the equipment I needed to enable me to do that.'

The support network, Disabled Staff in the Cabinet Office (DISCO), is particularly valuable for employees of the Civil Service, according to Vicky Waite. DISCO not only encourages staff to use relevant contacts, but enables them to contribute to future legislation. 'Rather than feeling like a victim, the network makes me feel creative and assertive.'

Employment

Making it work: managing disability in the workplace

Nick Goss works with a number of large companies consulting on disability employment issues. Here, he examines the issues facing employers.

As disability issues become an integral part of modern-day employment practice, many employers are adopting the view that any employment strategy based solely on complying with legislation is uneconomical, legally dangerous and fails to make real business sense.

There is also a growing realisation that employers who see disability employment issues as the sole concern of their human resources departments are leaving themselves open to a strategy that leads to underperformance and unnecessary expense, due to the lack of a co-ordinated approach.

Increasingly, companies who are successfully employing and retaining disabled people are doing so as part of their overall business plan. This often involves many different departments working together to identify what additional resources, policies and practices will be required to employ and retain the right person for the job, irrespective of disability.

Underpinning such a strategy is the need for common, measurable goals throughout the organisation, and increasing levels of disability awareness amongst all staff.

A good starting point is to have the disability employment strategy championed by an executive other than the Director of Human Resources. This sends a strong signal about the importance and breadth of the initiative, and brings with it a range of resources, which might otherwise be difficult to obtain.

For example, having a strategy which is led by a company's Head of Property Services or IT can bring immediate and tangible solutions to disability employment issues that relate to these departments.

Then there is the need to provide focused information and advice throughout a company on disability issues. As organisations become more disparate in nature, finding ways of delivering the right information at the right time becomes more challenging.

Increasingly, companies who are successfully employing and retaining disabled people are doing so as part of their overall business plan

---

Throughout the workplace, there is the need for a range of tools to manage disability-related issues. For example, tailor-made telephone support services, combined with web-based information provision, are innovative ways of supporting disabled staff.

These and other ways of providing staff with access to specific information, such as leaflets, videos, and CD-roms, can build confidence and develop trust around disability, as well as helping to avoid the legal pitfalls.

These tools can also assist line managers to work through specific disability-related issues via one-to-one or group coaching. Examples of issues that can be effectively explored using these techniques include managing mental health, and distinguishing between disability-related issues and those of general performance.

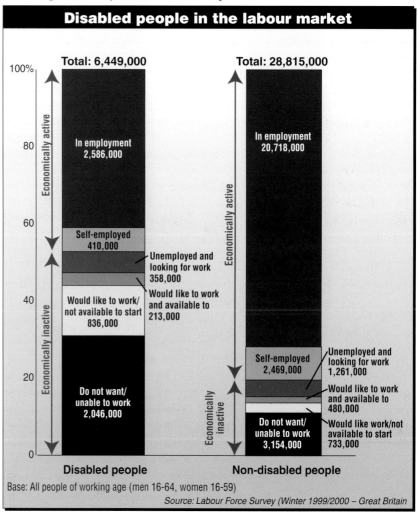

Disabled people in the labour market

Total: 6,449,000 — Disabled people
- Economically active
  - In employment 2,586,000
  - Self-employed 410,000
  - Unemployed and looking for work 358,000
  - Would like to work and available to start 213,000
- Economically inactive
  - Would like to work/not available to start 836,000
  - Do not want/unable to work 2,046,000

Total: 28,815,000 — Non-disabled people
- Economically active
  - In employment 20,718,000
  - Self-employed 2,469,000
  - Unemployed and looking for work 1,261,000
  - Would like to work and available to start 480,000
- Economically inactive
  - Would like work/not available to start 733,000
  - Do not want/unable to work 3,154,000

Base: All people of working age (men 16-64, women 16-59)

Source: Labour Force Survey (Winter 1999/2000 – Great Britain

However, the key to successful disability employment strategies is to place disabled people at the centre of the process. To achieve this, an environment of trust must be developed to enable disabled employees, and potential employees, to comment on and help develop the process.

Disabled people need to understand why an employer wants to know about disability issues within its organisation, and how

that information will be used. Employers need to make it clear that the process of consultation

will be outgoing and will lead to tangible outcomes. This can often be perceived as high risk but, as many companies have discovered, when it comes to disability, those who dare, win.

• The above information is from the *RADAR Bulletin*, produced by RADAR. See page 41 for address details.

© RADAR
June, 2001

Disability rights to cover millions more workers

The government yesterday promised the biggest extension of disability rights for 30 years, including legislation to protect people diagnosed with cancer and HIV from victimisation by their employers.

Margaret Hodge, the employment minister, said she would amend the Disability Discrimination Act to strengthen protection for 600,000 already in work and cover nearly 7m jobs previously excluded from the legislation.

They include police officers, firefighters and prison officers, but not the armed services, which are to remain exempt following a rearguard action by senior officers.

By 2004, small businesses will be obliged to make 'reasonable adjustments' to their premises for the benefit of disabled employees and job applicants.

All firms will have to remove unreasonable obstacles for disabled customers. And the government will place a legal duty on public bodies to provide equal opportunities for disabled people.

Bert Massie, chairman of the disability rights commission, said it was 'the most significant programme of reforms since disability rights legislation was first introduced 30 years ago . . . Under these proposals, millions more disabled people will be protected against discrimination.'

Ms Hodge said the changes – recommended by a taskforce in 1999

By John Carvel, Social Affairs Editor

– would give disabled people 'comprehensive and enforceable civil rights'.

Enhanced protection for cancer sufferers was triggered by evidence that women were sacked, or selected for redundancy, while the disease was in remission and unlikely to recur. In one case, a woman who had recovered from a mastectomy was told to quit when she needed reconstructive surgery.

By 2004, small businesses will be obliged to make 'reasonable adjustments' to their premises for the benefit of disabled employees and job applicants

Ms Hodge said: 'This is shameful. The taskforce found some employers discriminate against people diagnosed with cancer even though the cancer had no present effects, or was in remission.'

Under the new law, people's employment rights would be protected from the moment they were

diagnosed as likely to require substantial treatment for cancer or HIV. They would have the same rights as those available for those diagnosed with diabetes, epilepsy or arthritis.

Nick Partridge, chief executive of Terrence Higgins Trust Lighthouse, said: 'The announcement sends a clear message to employers that it is not acceptable to practise discrimination against people just because they have HIV.'

There will also be more protection for people who are blind or partially sighted, but have had difficulty qualifying as disabled.

Ms Hodge said she made no compromises to win business support for the changes.

'We have persuaded employers that nobody will be asked to do anything unaffordable or beyond common sense.'

The average cost for smaller firms making their premises suitable for disabled employees would be £78 per person.

The CBI said the 2004 deadline for small firms was 'appropriate and realistic'.

Paul Whitehouse, chairman of the Association of Chief Police Officers, welcomed the extension of the act. 'It will require us to establish clearly what the requirements are to be an effective police officer.'

© Guardian Newspapers Limited 2001

Disabled people as workers

Information from the Employers' Forum on Disability

- there are 6.2 million disabled people of working age in the UK, 18 per cent of the working population (Labour Force Survey summer 1998).
- disabled people in employment tend to work in a similar range of jobs to non-disabled people and can offer employers exactly the same range of skills and talents as anyone else. They often have additional problem-solving skills developed from managing their everyday life. Yet unemployment rates among people with disabilities are around two-and-a-half times those for non-disabled people.
- disabled people tend to be more loyal than many other workers and have a tendency to remain with employers for longer periods.
- disabled people have fewer days off sick and fewer days' absence for reasons other than illness compared to non-disabled workers, their productivity rates are on a par with other workers and they have better than average safety records.
- disabled employees have the same aspirations and ambitions as anyone else in the workforce. They want jobs which are challenging and rewarding and are just as likely to want opportunities for career development and promotion.
- 7 out of 10 economically active disabled people of working age will have become disabled during their working life. Losing the services of an employee who becomes disabled deprives organisations of a considerable asset and investment in terms of their skills and experience. It can also be very expensive. One large employer found that the average cost of retiring an employee on medical grounds was £40,000.
- 1 out of every 4 customers is disabled or has a disabled person in their immediate circle. The value of the disability market in the UK is estimated to be £40 billion per annum. Organisations that employ disabled people are better able to anticipate and respond to the needs of disabled customers. They have in their disabled employees an inbuilt source of information and advice about their potential customers on which they can draw in developing their marketing strategies.

• The above information is from the Employers' Forum on Disability's web site which can be found at www.employers-forum.co.uk

© The Employers' Forum on Disability

Disabled people and society

Stop harassing disabled people and start helping us to rejoin society. 'Don't waste taxpayers' money making sure that we haven't been miraculously cured'

By Mik Scarlet

So the Labour Government, fresh from its second landslide victory, has decided that it's time to bear down on the terrible scourge of disabled people – those scrounging terrors that are such a drain on society. People like me, perhaps. Now, I know that fraud within the benefit system is something that must be stamped out but, as a wheelchair user of 20 years, I do feel that Alistair Darling is picking on a group who are more innocent than most. I mean, I'm sure that the number of people faking it by pretending to be chronically physically or mentally disabled doesn't exactly threaten to destabilise the Government's finances.

In truth, there are two main problems with the idea that all the disabled people should be getting out there into work. First, although there are companies out there screaming for skilled staff, are they looking for people who have spent most of their adult life being left out of the workplace as a hidden statistic?

Despite what Mr Darling says, most disabled people who claim

Most disabled people looking for work are amazed if they get an interview, let alone the job

Incapacity Benefit are truly unable to work, whether it is through physical or mental limitations. They also did not attend schools where they gained the qualifications needed to find work. We are not the computer experts, the skilled managers and technicians that the modern workplace so desperately needs. No: we have mainly still been educated in the second-class system called 'special schools', where coping with incontinence is more important than maths and physics.

Even if we were lucky and had parents who fought to get us into mainstream education, with the result that we do have the much-needed skills, we still have to get over the prejudices of employers. How many times in the past have I applied for employment and been turned down even though I know I am properly qualified?

Most disabled people looking for work are amazed if they get an interview, let alone the job. If, by a miracle, we do get the position, we then have the problem of access to the workplace. An employer can get a government grant towards helping to make the physical adaptations to a building that would mean their new disabled employee could actually get into work, but this can take up to six months even to get started – not many employers will give a new employee over six months before they start work.

So finding work can be just like wheeling up Mount Everest for a disabled person, even when found fit enough to work. But then are we even going to be considered for those 'plum' jobs? Are we going to get on to the 'career path'? Or are we, more likely, heading for a dead-end job, the kind that most people dream of getting out of? But then at least it would get us out of the house! Even if we are employed, and the building we work in is accessible, and the job is in a career that will lead to success, we still do not enjoy the same legal employment rights as every other person in that firm.

This is the second problem. The equal rights act passed for the disabled still means that, if we face discrimination, it is we disabled people, and not the Government, who have to take the offending company to court. We never get the 'Queen versus' when we face discrimination. The Disabled Rights Commission will finance the prosecution and help us with legal arguments, but in the end we have to take the prosecution to court ourselves.

All other groups protected by equal rights legislation will have any legal battles pursued by the Crown, since to discriminate against them is a criminal act. But not for us, no. When we're spat at in the street, or told we're not welcome in a restaurant, or sacked for having more than two days off sick (it has happened to me – you see, employers believe that any sick leave means that a disabled employee is about to become a sickly, crippled drain on his company, one that needs getting rid of) – then it is a civil offence, not a crime against society.

And here lies the root of why disabled people are so fed up with being picked on when benefit reform rears its ugly head.

I hoped I would one day live in a world with accessible buildings, tolerant people and the chance to show the talents I know I have in the workplace

---

When my spine collapsed 20 years ago and I had to go into a wheelchair, I hoped then for a future where one day I would be equal to my able-bodied fellow citizens. I hoped I would one day live in a world with accessible buildings, tolerant people and the chance to show the talents I know I have in the workplace. Ha. Here I am, having grown up in my wheelchair, living in a world where I am still not truly equal, watching what little rights I did have slowly being whittled away.

Even the disabled parking badge is becoming a joke. In London, where I live, some boroughs have their own badge, and this means that your average disabled person has to drive round for hours trying and praying to find one of the few spaces for normal badge holders. And, of course, it's not like we can use public transport. No, the plan to make public transport fully accessible means that I'll be over 70 when I can get on a bus.

Maybe if society treated us as part of it, we might be more open to the penny-pinching ways of successive politicians. Stop wasting money making sure we haven't been miraculously cured (that only happens in TV soap operas), and spend that cash on ensuring that buildings are accessible, making sure disabled people are treated as equal in society, and making sure that schools are fully integrated. Then you won't have a disabled underclass that you have now, that costs so much of your hard-earned taxes to be paid over in benefits. Or then you can waste billions on helping the Americans with 'Son of Star Wars', or the Millennium Dome, or other fantastically cost-effective projects.

One last thing, and this applies to us all, equally. Always remember that the health of a society lies in the ways it treats those who are most needy.

Left out

A ground-breaking new survey looking at the accessibility of Britain to disabled people. It also offers advice to campaigners and organisations on how to improve access to a wide range of goods, services and facilities.

In September 1999 we launched our 'Left Out' campaign – a campaign to make Britain more accessible to disabled people. We started the campaign because of the amount of calls we were receiving from people who had been turned away from shops, restaurants, cinemas or public buildings because they were inaccessible or because of the attitude of staff.

At the start of October the Left Out posters were distributed across the country. They had a tremendous effect with hundreds of people contacting us and offering help. Over several months, 350 disability campaigners completed detailed access surveys on a wide range of buildings and services. Every kind of public building was covered. There were high street shops, restaurants, pubs, clubs, libraries and council buildings. The survey aimed to highlight both access problems and examples of good practice.

This grassroots research forms the basis for Scope's new report. The report highlights how organisations can work with disabled people to improve the accessibility of goods, facilities and services. It also offers advice to disability campaigners on how they can improve access locally.

Access is considered in its broadest context and includes issues like staff training, queue design, lifts and the style of e-commerce sites. Well-known high street brands are mentioned in the report and disabled people give their own access stories.

The report provides a snapshot of how businesses and other organisations are facing up to the challenges of the Disability Discrimination Act and urges UK plc to ensure their services are accessible to Britain's 8.6 million disabled people.

Left Out's main findings

- 76 per cent of respondents could find no evidence that parking bays for disabled people were being checked by staff.
- 37 per cent of designated parking bays were being used by non-disabled drivers.
- 64 per cent of buildings had an entrance with level access.
- 30 per cent of the premises had automatic doors.
- 30 per cent of the businesses surveyed had customer information available in a format other than standard print.
- 21 per cent of facilities had hearing loops.
- 17 per cent of staff were not

Some businesses have realised that finding ways to end discrimination will lead to an increase in customers

respectful towards disabled people.
- 53 per cent of venues did not have an accessible toilet.

The survey revealed that disabled people continue to face access discrimination. Not surprisingly physical access was a problem, there were steps everywhere, counters were too high and corridors and doors not wide enough. But there was also a problem with people's attitude to disability.

Since December 1996 it has been illegal (under the Disability Discrimination Act) to refuse to serve someone because they are disabled. Yet disabled customers are still being turned away. One respondent was told a restaurant was full despite the fact that there were only two tables were being used.

From October last year new provisions under the Disability Discrimination Act have been in

What are the characteristics of disabled drivers?

Comparison of key characteristics

%	Disabled motorists*	Orange badge holders	All motorists†
Men	63	67	58
Women	37	33	42
Age 65+	23	36	16
Working	6	8	62
Drive every day/most days	81	81	87
Current cars per household	1.29	1.37	1.57
Projected cars per household in two years' time	1.30	1.26	1.62
Ideal number of cars per household	1.53	1.53	1.92
Average age of cars (years)	1.8	6.6	7.8
Expected length of ownership (years)	2.8	5.5	4.7
Average mileage	7,800	6,500	10,000

Base: † All motorists (1,373)/ * Disabled motorists (104)

Source: RAC Report on Motoring 2001

force, so now shopkeepers and theatre managers alike should be making 'reasonable adjustments' to ensure their premises and services are accessible to disabled people.

Many of the adjustments are simple and inexpensive. Large-print menus or chairs available if people are expected to queue for some time do not take much effort. Often it just takes a bit of thought. Having straws available in pubs can make life easier for some people, and more and more places of worship are installing induction loops and buying large-print hymn books.

The survey did not just find examples of bad practice. There were many survey forms that reported excellent service and facilities for disabled people. Some businesses have realised that finding ways to end discrimination will lead to an increase in customers. Santa Fe, a restaurant in North London, not only introduced large-print menus but they also have what's on offer on a small tape recorder. Many theatres have signed performances and audio-visual displays are increasingly common in some museums.

The Post Office has now recognised the importance of developing a queuing system incorporating seating for those unable to stand for very long. Although waiting time might not be any shorter the Post Office is designing a new system to ensure queuing in future is accessible.

At Christmas campaigner Trevor Dobson surveyed five department stores on Oxford Street. John Lewis, which came out top, had invested in disability equality training for all staff as well as having customer information in a range of formats.

B&Q seems to be embracing the disabled community to get its share of the disabled person's pound. In some stores there are even scooters to help people with mobility impairments get around. Other businesses are recognising the business case for ensuring premises and the service offered are accessible. Many survey respondents have indicated that businesses that are inaccessible are losing out on custom to those which are able to meet the needs of disabled shoppers.

However, some businesses are prevented from making physical changes to buildings by local authorities. Ensuring managers in planning and highways departments understand the needs of disabled customers is crucial: at the moment too many planning applications to make a building entrance accessible are being turned down.

Other businesses are recognising the business case for ensuring premises and the service offered are accessible

---

The actual access to a building or the service within is only part of the picture. Accessibility of public transport or the availability of parking should also be taken into account.

Some campaigners reported successes with more dropped kerbs and finding other external access solutions. Local access groups, access officers and MPs have secured improvements to town centres but new trends mean new issues to tackle. Pedestrianisation schemes with little or no parking for disabled people present a huge challenge to those who cannot walk very far.

The same problem exists in large out-of-town shopping centres or supermarkets which might appear really accessible. Yet blocked aisles and the distance needed to travel to find the products which need to be purchased creates 'access' obstacles. Tesco in Cheshunt has eased this problem by making scooters available free of charge to customers.

But we have to wait until 2004 before the Disability Discrimination Act starts to defend disabled people's rights in terms of physical access. In the meantime thousands of premises are 'off limits' to wheelchair users and others with mobility impairments. Many disabled people continue to do their banking or collect a pension on the high street.

As campaigners our job is to ensure buildings, services and products are accessible to all. But with the DDA framed as it is, we will need to find solutions other than just encouraging individuals to take cases through the courts. Pressure will need to be put on politicians to improve the legislation, but we also need to get the message through to businesses that they will lose customers unless they become accessible.

In March the Centre for Accessible Environments is setting up a register of access consultants. 020 7357 8182. For more information contact campaigns@scope.org.uk

• For a copy of *Left Out* please send a cheque made payable to 'Scope' for £3.30 (individuals) and £22 (organisations) – the cost includes postage & packing – to the Library & Information Unit, Scope, 6 Market Road, London N7 9PW.

© *Scope*

And the survey shows . . .

The majority of disabled motorists would struggle to manage with public transport no matter how much the service was improved, a major report has revealed.

The RAC report on *Motoring 2001*, published by RAC Motoring Services, showed that the willingness of car drivers to use public transport has slumped to an eight-year low. This is particularly disappointing in light of the government's 10-year £180 billion package to invest in rail, roads and local transport in a bid to reduce traffic congestion by the year 2010.

Difficult

Nearly all disabled motorists stated they would find it 'very difficult' to adjust their lifestyle to being without a car – compared to 86 per cent of able-bodied motorists.

There are an estimated two million disabled drivers in this country – a third of whom use wheelchairs. Of these, two-thirds said they do not use public transport because it simply does not meet their needs.

Douglas Campbell, Executive Director of the Disabled Drivers' Association, said: 'No matter how much they improve public transport it won't have a major impact on car usage by disabled people because it still won't provide a door-to-door service which is so essential for disabled people.'

Upgraded

However, the RAC report suggests that although improved facilities for disabled drivers on public transport are unlikely to have a great impact on getting disabled drivers to switch from their cars, it is important that buses and trains, bus stops, stations and interchange locations are continually upgraded with disabled people in mind because of the large number of people with disabilities who do not have a car.

In the report, disabled drivers said they felt strongly that without a car they would lose their sense of freedom and their ability to shop or to visit relatives. They specifically mentioned the loss of independence and inability to get to vital appointments, such as the hospital, dentist, etc.

Motorists surveyed by the RAC did an average 10,000 miles per year – 3,000 more than the average disabled motorist. Mr Campbell believed this was largely due to disabled drivers finding it increasingly difficult to afford to do the extent of motoring they would like to.

Parking

The survey also revealed that 81 per cent of disabled motorists used their car daily, compared to 87 per cent of able-bodied drivers. Parking problems were the bane of the life of the disabled drivers, with nearly half calling for more parking spaces.

Disabled drivers also felt strongly that there was misuse of the orange/blue badge system and that there should be severe penalties for illegal parking in disabled parking spaces – suggesting that offending drivers should be fined up to £1,000 or have penalty points added to their licences. Despite the provision of dedicated parking bays for disabled motorists and the ability to park for free and on yellow lines in most places, disabled motorists still had trouble finding a parking space.

Spaces

The report showed that only 38 per cent of disabled drivers found a space within five minutes and another 24 per cent within 10 minutes – compared to 53 per cent of all motorists finding a space within five minutes and 32 per cent within 10 minutes.

Mr Campbell was interested to note that a staggering 88 per cent of disabled motorists felt strongly that there was a misuse of orange badges and said it was frustrating to see people using badges that didn't belong to them.

• The above information is an extract from *The Magic Carpet*, the publication of the Disabled Drivers' Association. See page 41 for their address details.

© *The Disabled Drivers' Association Summer 2001*

Use of public transport

%	Car		Buses or coaches		Train/underground	
	Disabled motorists	All motorists	Disabled motorists*	All motorists	Disabled motorists*	All motorists
Travel to/from work	11	51	3	4	3	5
Travel in connection with your work	11	25	0	2	0	6
Visiting family and friends	92	87	11	5	16	7
Going shopping	95	90	24	9	5	9
Going to sports/leisure/entertainment	57	60	14	7	8	9
Taking children to school/group	14	25	0	1	0	0
Never use it	0	0	59	81	76	75

Base: All motorists (1,563)/ Disabled motorists (104)/ *Those able to use public transport (37)

Source: RAC Report on Motoring 2000/2001

Disability issues

Information from Scope

Background

Numbers of disabled people

We cannot be certain about the number of disabled people in Great Britain. However, the OPCS surveys[1] published in 1988 estimated that there were 5.8 million disabled adults (over the age of 16) living in Great Britain and 360,000 disabled children.

This meant that one in four households in Great Britain had at least one member with a disability. However the latest Government research[2] estimates that there are considerably more disabled people, placing the number at 8.6 million disabled adults living in private households, i.e. 1 in 5 of the adult population.

The number is likely to rise further with an increasingly elderly population, as the likelihood of disability increases with age.

Discrimination and attitudes

Disabled people continue to face discrimination and difficulties imposed by society in every area of their lives. The common experiences of disabled people are of rejection and enormous difficulty in taking part in even the most ordinary activities such as shopping, going to the cinema or to the pub.

Discrimination is present in education and employment, leading to lifelong dependence on welfare benefits.

Many polling stations are inaccessible, therefore disabled people are denied the right to vote on equal terms with non-disabled people. In addition, disabled people are forced into dependence, suffer humiliation and struggle with an inaccessible environment every day.

As a consequence many disabled people give up the struggle of attempting to take part in society and stay at home.

The exclusion of disabled people from society means that some non-disabled people have never met a disabled person and therefore do not have the opportunity to develop opinions and attitudes about them based on personal experience.

Lack of awareness and fear of the unknown is compounded by the predominantly negative media images of disabled people and of disability generally. For example in a survey conducted by the Leonard Cheshire Foundation[3] nearly one-third of people questioned thought that wheelchair-users were 'less intelligent'; and 44 per cent of opinion leaders thought that using a wheelchair would present a major obstacle to gaining employment. Such misconceptions lead to a vicious circle of rejection, discrimination and exclusion.

Language

The language we use reflects the way we think. It also shapes the way we think. The language we use about disability is an important way of influencing our own and society's attitudes.

Words and phrases to avoid include: handicapped person, spastic, wheelchair-bound, sufferer, the disabled.

Use the following instead: disabled person, has cerebral palsy, wheelchair-user, has an impairment.

Social versus medical model of disability

Behaviour towards disabled people is governed by the picture or 'model' of disability that others carry in their minds. These models, in turn, affect the way in which society is organised.

The two main models are:
• The medical model – this sees

disability as an illness, and disabled people as patients in need of a cure so that they can fit into 'normal' society. The emphasis is on the condition rather than the person.

- The social model – this recognises disabled people as equals who are battling against very unequal odds – i.e. society's attitudes. The emphasis is on society's responsibilities and changing attitudes rather than the disabled person's problem.

Education/inclusion

Discrimination against disabled people begins from the moment they are born. Disabled children are often segregated, with medical considerations predominating, undermining a wider approach and the possibility of enjoying a normal life alongside non-disabled peers.

Early school experiences (positive or negative) can have a profound impact on how disabled people feel about themselves and influence expectations about their future role in society.

Meanwhile, the controversy over special schools continues. Some people argue that whilst special segregated education exists, most non-disabled children never come into contact with disabled children. Their attitudes therefore are formed from the attitudes of adults and the media, perpetuating negative attitudes and stereotyping. Disabled and non-disabled children learning and growing up together takes away the fear of the unknown and makes disability part of the norm.

- 99 per cent of all children are educated in mainstream schools.
- Around 1.5 million children (18 per cent of pupils) in schools in England are identified as having Special Educational Needs (SEN). Primary schools have a slightly higher proportion (19 per cent) than secondary schools (17 per cent).
- From 1993-98 the total number of pupils in special schools remained constant at around 98,000.

- Of pupils with SEN Statements, 58 per cent are now educated in maintained mainstream schools (a rise from 48 per cent since 1993), 39 per cent in special schools (maintained and non-maintained) or Pupil Referral Units, and 3 per cent in independent schools.

Figures underline a long-term trend towards greater inclusion of disabled pupils in mainstream schools, with a corresponding drop in the percentage in special schools (down from 49 per cent in 1992).

There is a wide variation across Local Education Authorities in the percentage of pupils in special schools. (Figures taken from School Censuses January 1997 and 1998.)

Employment

Many employers still favour non-disabled applicants over disabled people. This happens for a variety of reasons ranging from fear or prejudice to misunderstandings about people's abilities or the supposed costs of employing a disabled person.

Whilst some major companies are instigating equal opportunities there are still instances of prejudice among fellow employees against disabled colleagues. Once in employment disabled people do not have the same promotion prospects as able-bodied colleagues or have to work harder to maintain their position within the organisation.

- Disabled people are only half as likely as non-disabled people to be in employment. When employed, they are 6 per cent

more likely to work part-time. Their likelihood of being long-term unemployed is also higher.[4]

- Of those looking for work, 62 per cent of disabled people felt that they had been refused a job or interview because of their disability and 85 per cent thought that employers were reluctant to offer them jobs because of their disability.[5]
- Disabled people are six times more likely to face discrimination when applying for a job than their able-bodied counterparts.[6]
- 35 per cent of disabled people had been unable to accept a job offer because the building was inaccessible.[7]

Goods and services

In Scope's *Disabled In Britain* report[8], one in three disabled people said they had been refused service in a public place such as a cinema, restaurant, pub/club, theatre, sporting event or leisure centre. The Disability Discrimination Act (see below) has acted as a catalyst for commercial and public sector providers of goods and services to improve physical access as part of their service to disabled people as reported in Scope's research report, *In Good Company?*[9]

Families/carers

In 1995, Scope published the results of its study into carers' lives – one of the largest studies ever undertaken – in *Disabled in Britain: behind closed doors – the carers' experience.*[10]

The needs of different families and carers differ widely, and may reflect partly the type of support available to them, and partly the needs of the person for whom they care (ranging from young carers and young disabled children, to elderly carers and elderly relatives being cared for). Here, we are only able to give a partial picture of the needs of some families/carers.

Emotional/ psychological needs

Carers, whether family, relations or friends, play a crucial role in the lives of disabled people. As well as being a potentially rewarding and satisfying role, caring for disabled

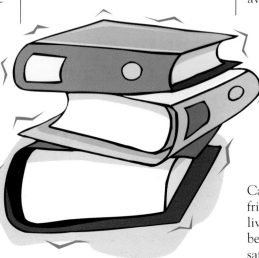

people is very often stressful and undervalued[11], in economic and status terms and in terms of its central role in supporting disabled people.

Caring for a disabled person also affects other members of the family, especially siblings. Parents may feel guilty for not giving enough time to siblings, and siblings may harbour feelings of resentment about the lack of time parents give to them. Three-quarters of respondents in Scope's 1995 survey[10] who cared for disabled children between six and 15 felt they were sometimes neglecting other family members (as opposed to 50 per cent who cared for someone aged 65 or more).

Physical needs

Caring for a person with a disability can be hard work. Many carers feel both physically tired and mentally fatigued because of the effort involved in obtaining and providing the services needed. Carers often put their own health and safety at risk through physical activity necessitated by lack of equipment, or through the mental worries brought about by the constant anxiety.

Financial/economic needs

'Caring costs', said Scope's 1995 report on caring.[12] It found that many respondents bear many of the costs themselves: their careers suffer, they experience financial hardship and are frequently stressed and unwell.

Legislation

In 1995 instead of full, enforceable civil rights legislation the Conservative Government introduced the Disability Discrimination Act 1995 (DDA).

The parts of the Act are as follows:
- Part I Definition of disability (i.e. who is covered by the Act).
- Part II Employment – prohibiting discrimination in relation to recruitment, training, benefits, management practices, etc. in trade organisations and contract work. Currently, this does not apply to companies with fewer than 16 employees.
- Part III Goods and services – requiring service providers and

those selling, letting or managing premises to enable disabled people to make use of their goods, facilities and services.
- Part IV Education – Special requirements are outlined for amending existing education legislation and providing other duties in relation to information for disabled people.
- Part V Transport – providing the Secretary of State with powers to establish a minimum access criteria for new transport vehicles to be phased in over time.
- Part VI National Disability Council – requires this to be set up and details its duties and powers.
- Part VII Miscellaneous issues – including the restriction of publicity, government appointments, regulations and interpretation.

Goods and services

Since December 1996, it has been unlawful for service providers and those responsible for selling, letting or managing premises to refuse service, to provide a worse standard of service or to offer a service on worse terms to disabled people. Further provisions require service providers to make reasonable steps to:
- a) Amend policies, procedures and practices which make it impossible or unreasonably difficult for disabled people to access the service from October 1999 (e.g. a no dogs policy in cases where visually impaired people wish to enter the premises with a guide dog).
- b) Provide auxiliary aids and services where this would enable or facilitate disabled people's use

of a service from October 1999 (e.g. lifting items off shelves in shops for those unable to manage alone).
- c) Overcome physical features which
- make it impossible or unreasonably difficult for disabled people to use a service, by providing the service by a reasonable alternative method from October 1999.
- amend or remove physical feature(s) of the premises which make it impossible or unreasonably difficult for disabled people to use a service or provide a reasonable means of avoiding it from 2004.

References and further reading
1. OPCS surveys of Disability in Great Britain. Reports 1-6. HMSO, 1988
2. Grundy et al. *Disability in Great Britain*. DSS/Corporate Document Services, 1999
3. Knight, J. & Brent, M. *Access Denied: Disabled People's Experience of Social Exclusion*. Leonard Cheshire, 1998
4. *Labour Force Survey*, Winter 1997/98
5. Lamb, B. & Layzell, S. *Disabled in Britain: A World Apart*. Scope, 1994
6. Graham, & Lamb, B. *An Equal Chance or No Chance*, The Spastics Society, 1987
7. Lamb, B. & Layzell, S. Op. cit.
8. Ibid
9. Stewart, J. *In Good Company?* Scope, 1996
10. Lamb, B. & Layzell, S. *Disabled in Britain: behind closed doors*. Scope, 1995
11. *Eight hours a day and taken for granted?* The Princess Royal Trust for Carers, 1998
12. Stewart, J. Op. cit.

- For any additional information relating to cerebral palsy, Scope and its activities, please send an A4 stamped (40p) addressed envelope to: Scope, Cerebral Palsy Helpline, PO Box 833, Milton Keynes, MK12 5NY.

The Information Services Department acknowledges the help and support of everyone who has been involved in the production of this information.

What is a learning disability?

Information from the Foundation for People with Learning Disabilities

Summary

- People with learning disabilities find it harder to learn, but they can do so with help from other people
- People usually have a learning disability from birth or sometimes from early childhood
- People with learning disabilities are not all the same. They have different needs, come from all kinds of families and have varied lives
- Some people have severe learning disabilities and will need a lot of day-to-day support. Others have mild or moderate learning disabilities and can live with much less help from other people
- Some people prefer to say learning difficulties instead of learning disabilities

If someone has a learning disability it means that they may not learn things as quickly as other people and they may need more help and support to learn. Learning disability is not an illness. It is a permanent condition, but with the right kind of help many people can acquire practical and social skills even if this may take them longer than usual.

Learning disability is nearly always present from birth, though this is sometimes not recognised until children fail to reach milestones in their development such as sitting up or beginning to talk.

Like the rest of the population, people with learning disabilities have very diverse personalities and characteristics. People's backgrounds and family circumstances will also vary and these, together with the nature and degree of disability, will help to determine what it means for a particular person to have a learning disability.

The nature of people's dis-abilities varies widely and will affect the kind of support they may require. Someone with a learning disability finds it more difficult to understand new or complicated information. They also find it harder than other people to learn new skills. These may be practical things like tying shoelaces or social skills such as holding a conversation. Some people may not speak and need to find other ways of communicating with those around them. Some need help with everyday things like getting dressed or making a cup of tea. Others will live quite independently with much less assistance.

Most carers, professionals and service providers refer to 'learning disabilities', but some self-advocates in UK organisations like People First prefer to describe themselves as having 'learning difficulties', and some professionals also use this term. 'Intellectual disabilities' is commonly used internationally, although in the USA, the term 'developmental disabilities' is also used.

Many people believe that using any terms like 'learning disabilities' is stigmatising. At the same time, it would be difficult to organise services and support if there was no way of defining the people for whom they were being provided.

> *If someone has a learning disability it means that they may not learn things as quickly as other people and they may need more help and support to learn*

More information about learning disabilities

British Institute of Learning Disabilities (BILD)
Wolverhampton Road, Kidderminster, Worcestershire DY10 3PP,

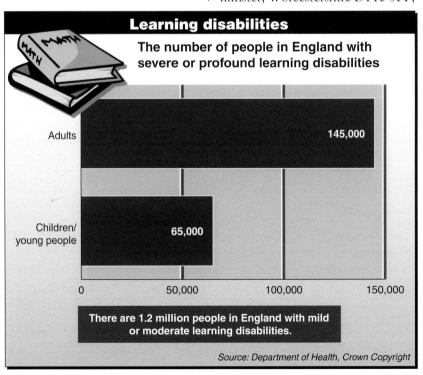

Learning disabilities

The number of people in England with severe or profound learning disabilities

- Adults: 145,000
- Children/young people: 65,000

(scale: 0, 50,000, 100,000, 150,000)

There are 1.2 million people in England with mild or moderate learning disabilities.

Source: Department of Health, Crown Copyright

United Kingdom. Tel: 01562 850 251. Fax: 01562 851 970. Email: bild@bild.org.uk Web site: www.bild.org.uk

Department of Health

Learning Disabilities: UK government website covering learning disabilities, with links, news, and publications on the subject. Web site: www.doh.gov.uk/learningdisabilities

Foundation for People with Learning Disabilties

20-21 Cornwall Terrace, London NW1 4QL, United Kingdom. Tel: 020 7535 7400. E-mail: fpld@fpld.org.uk Web site:

www.learningdisabilities.org.uk Provides range of information on learning disabilities via its website.

Mencap

123 Golden Lane, London EC1Y 0RT, United Kingdom. Tel: 020 7454 0454. Fax: 020 7696 5540. E-mail: Information@mencap.org.uk Web site: www.mencap.org.uk Largest provider of services for people with learning disabilities within England, Northern Ireland and Wales.

LD Online

Extremely comprehensive US website covering all aspects of

learning disabilities. Web site: www.ldonline.org/index.html

Publications

Learning Disabilities: The Fundamental Facts. Foundation for People with Learning Disabilities, 2000. 54 pages. All the latest facts and figures on learning disabilities in the United Kingdom.

• The Foundation for People with Learning Disabilities is a registered charity which works to improve the quality of life for people with learning disabilities. See page 41 for their address details.

© The Foundation for People with Learning Disabilities

British Institute of Learning Disabilities

What do we mean by people with a learning disability?

In many ways people with learning disabilities are the same as everyone else. They have rights; responsibilities; fall in love; want to be alone; want to be in a crowd; become parents; grieve their losses; just like everyone else on the planet. The only difference is that people with learning disabilities have more difficulty than other people with activities that involve thinking and understanding.

For some people these difficulties are very slight and make little difference to their ability to live an ordinary life but people with more severe learning disabilities will need extra help and support with their everyday lives. Some people with a learning disability may also have an additional impairment such as a sensory impairment or a physical disability.

They may have a dual diagnosis of learning disability and mental illness or they may need help to control certain aspects of their behaviour.

Many people with learning disabilities achieve a great deal in their lives. Some people have become excellent actors or sportsmen and women. Other people run a business

bild

or have a career. Many people now have jobs, something that would not have been contemplated 20 years ago.

Where do people with learning disabilities live?

In the past many people with learning disabilities lived in large hospitals or institutions. In the UK most of these large institutions have now closed and those that are left are offering a different type of service. People with learning disabilities now live in a variety of settings in ordinary neighbourhoods.

Some people live with their families; others live in groups with other people with a learning disability; some will live alone. People who need more support might live in a situation where they have a landlady to help them or paid staff living with them.

―――――

Many people with learning disabilities achieve a great deal in their lives

How many people in the UK have a learning disability?

It is estimated that 1.2 million people in the UK have a learning disability, and for 200,000 people the disability will be severe.

Learning disability affects all social classes and all races.

Global terminology

In the UK we use the term Learning Disability or Learning Difficulty.

Other countries world-wide use different terms:
• USA uses Mental Retardation or Developmental Disability
• Australia uses Intellectual Impairment
• Other countries use Mental Handicap

• BILD is an independent registered charity based in Kidderminster, UK. Since the organisation was founded in 1972 BILD has been committed to improving the quality of life of all people with a learning disability. The above information is an extract from BILD's web site which can be found at www.bild.org.uk Alternatively, please see page 41 for their address details.

© British Institute of Learning Disabilities (BILD)

How many people have learning disabilities?

Information from the Foundation for People with Learning Disabilities

Summary

- It is hard to work out exactly how many people have learning disabilities in the UK. There are between 230,000 and 350,000 people with severe learning disabilities and between 580,000 and 1,750,000 with milder learning disabilities.
- More males than females have severe learning disabilities.
- Mild learning disabilities are more common among males and people whose families are very poor or who have other problems.

There are no reliable official statistics for the total numbers of people in the UK who have learning disabilities. Government departments currently do not collect this information and any statistics would be unlikely to include those people with mild learning disabilities who do not use specialist learning disability services and who live more or less independently in the community.

Despite this lack of official data, reviews of prevalence studies in Europe, North America and Australia have produced broadly consistent results. Studies including only those people with learning disabilities known to service providers have found 3-4 people with severe learning disabilities in every 1,000 of the general population. Other studies which have screened whole populations have found somewhat higher rates: 6 per 1,000 of the overall population.

On this basis, in the UK there are an estimated:

- 230,000-350,000 people with severe learning disabilities
- 580,000-1,750,000 people with mild learning disabilities.

The overall numbers of people with learning disabilities vary according to gender, age, ethnic background and socio-economic circumstances.

In the UK severe learning disabilities are more common among:

- boys and men (possibly because of gender-linked genetic factors);
- younger people (because of above-average mortality rates for older people)

The overall numbers of people with learning disabilities varies according to gender, age, ethnic background and socio-economic circumstances

---

Mild learning disabilities are more common among:

- boys and men;
- younger people (because mortality rates are higher than the general population);
- people who live in poverty;
- people from adverse or unstable backgrounds.
- The Foundation for People with Learning Disabilities is a registered charity which works to improve the quality of life for people with learning disabilities. See page 41 for their address details.

© The Foundation for People with Learning Disabilities

Mencap research points to the public's double standards

By Lorna Duckworth, Social Affairs Correspondent

Only one in 14 adults with learning disabilities has a job, although most people in Britain think they are employable, a survey reveals today.

Research by the charity Mencap shows that people with learning disabilities still face discrimination, exclusion and prejudice even though the public claims to be supportive.

There are 1.4 million people in Britain whose development has been impaired by lifelong conditions such as Down's syndrome, autism or other forms of brain damage. Mencap's survey found that nine out of 10 Britons believe people with learning difficulties are employable. But while most would like to work, fewer than 90,000 have jobs and most of those are part-time.

Similarly, nearly all respondents said people with learning disabilities should have equal priority for medical treatment. But the charity says doctors are withholding or imposing treatment. Only 3 per cent of women with a learning disorder receive cervical cancer screening, some women have been bullied into sterilisation and many Down's sufferers have been denied heart surgery.

Most of the 1,066 people interviewed for the survey said they knew someone with a learning disability and would be happy to be their neighbour.

This apparent acceptance does not match reality, the charity says. Abuse is widespread and 90 per cent of people with a learning disorder were bullied in the past year.

© 2001 The Independent Newspaper (UK) Ltd

Inclusive education

Information from Barnardo's

Barnardo's believes that all young children, whatever their difficulty or level of ability, should be able to attend their local mainstream school.

To achieve inclusion, the education system needs to adapt to cater for a wide spectrum of ability and need. The development of inclusion is an ongoing process, the overall aim of which is to embrace diversity, rather than simply to tolerate differences.

Most young people benefit from remaining in mainstream education, with appropriate support where necessary. However, Barnardo's recognises that currently for a small number of children with very complex needs, education within a separate, supported environment is a positive option.

Key points

- A good education is important for all young people, in particular children with special educational needs and those from disadvantaged backgrounds
- Children educated outside the mainstream tend to achieve less academically, have less confidence and self-esteem, and are ill-prepared for adult life
- Without qualifications, young people have limited access to further education and little chance of finding a job in an already competitive employment market
- Fewer than one in 10 children with special educational needs attend a mainstream school[1]
- Inclusive education helps children and adults to develop a strong awareness of diversity, and promotes respect, understanding and co-operation
- Mainstream education provision should offer the full range of support and specialist services necessary to give all children access to a broad and balanced curriculum

- Inclusive education is a process involving changes in the way schools are organised, in the curriculum and in teaching strategies to accommodate the range of needs and abilities among pupils
- Segregated education is expensive. The same resources could be gradually redeployed into support and facilities which enable all children to be educated together.

Background

Every child has the right to a good education. Education is central to all other life experiences for young people. An incomplete or substandard education means fewer job opportunities and less chance of becoming independent. Young people who lack education are left ill-equipped for life.

One in ten young people leave school at 16 without qualifications. Many of these young people are likely to be those who have been in the care system, those who have been excluded from school or in segregated education, young disabled people and those with emotional, social and behavioural difficulties.[2] Without a good education, a young person's choices at 16 are limited. Youth employment is already high, at almost twice the rate than for the general population.

The past 15 years has seen major changes in education. Local management of schools has meant increased competition among schools, while as centralised funds have decreased there has been little available for specialist support services. Research suggests that the introduction of market forces into education has put pupils who are considered more costly to support at a disadvantage.[3]

Children with special educational needs

The category of special educational needs (SEN) includes children with physical, sensory and mental impairments (learning disabilities), those with learning difficulties (such as dyslexia) and children who have emotional and behavioural problems.

Just under three per cent of schoolchildren (282,000) have a

Numbers of children with disabilities

Numbers of children with disabilities by severity and age group, UK

Severity category	Children under 5	Children 5-15
I	19,872	38,649
II	19,872	71,777
III	2,760	22,085
IV	5,520	11,043
V	2,760	19,324
VI	1,656	38,649
VII	2,760	13,803
VIII		22,085
IX		13,803
X		11,043
Total	55,200	276,064

Source: Quality Protects: Disabled Children, Numbers and Categories, Department of Health, 2000

statement of special educational need. The number of children with statements has risen by 35 per cent in the past five years.[4]

More than 92 per cent of children with SEN are in special schools in the UK. In1998/99 there were just under 10 million children of school age in the UK, of whom 115,000 were in special schools.[1] For many disabled children, education in a mainstream setting is not even considered as an option.

There is a wide variation in response between different LEAs. In 1992, two authorities surveyed placed just one child in 200 in special schools. Three other authorities placed five times as many in special schools.[5] This is unfair to families, who should be able to expect national legislation to be implemented consistently in different parts of the country.

However, families often find that special school provision is not available near their homes. Catchment areas for many special schools are 100 square miles, and many LEAs export their children out of the area on the grounds that they cannot meet their needs locally. This results in many children facing long journeys to and from school each day.

Special schooling for disabled children has been criticised as focusing most on a child's care needs, at the expense of a high quality education. One report revealed that almost half the pupils in special schools were not receiving satisfactorily broad and balanced lessons.[6]

The government has placed strong emphasis on social inclusion, and has urged local education authorities to meet the needs of children with SEN in mainstream schools wherever possible.

Legislation expected in 2001 is likely to strengthen the right of disabled children to a place in mainstream school, and will establish parent partnership schemes in all local authorities to support disabled children and their families in the education system. However, it is likely that children with severe behavioural difficulties or mental impairments will continue to be excluded from mainstream schools where the will to include them does not exist.

What is inclusive education?
Inclusive education can be defined as:

> The process by which a school attempts to respond to all pupils as individuals by reconsidering and restructuring its curricular organisa-tion and provision and allocating resources to enhance equality of opportunity. Through this process, the school builds its capacity to accept all pupils from the local community who wish to attend and, in so doing, reduces the need to exclude pupils.[7]

The terms 'inclusion' and 'integration' are often used interchangeably, but they have different meanings. When a child is integrated, there may be specialist support provided, but there isn't the expectation that the system or institution itself should adapt.

The emphasis with inclusion is on developing systems which see diversity as positive and are responsive to this, rather than trying to make everyone fit in with what is available. Adopting an inclusive approach means that the structure, systems and environment of institutions have to change to accommodate a wide range of individual needs and levels of ability.

Barnardo's is committed to inclusive education as growing

evidence points to its educational and social benefits. Children with special educational needs show higher levels of academic attainment in mainstream schooling, and pupils who do not have identified difficulties appear to do as well in inclusive settings as in non-inclusive ones. Research shows that they also do better.[7]

Studies also show that attitudes of both staff and pupils towards people with special needs change when they have the opportunity to be part of the same school community, that there is increased understanding and co-operation between pupils of different abilities, and the development of positive relationships.[7]

Inclusive education is commonly thought to be expensive, but a report by the Audit Commission found that it was no more expensive to educate a child with learning disabilities in a mainstream school with support, than in a special school.[8] Spending on special education was nearly £1.7 billion in 1997/98, which is almost 5% of total education expenditure.[1] What is expensive for a local authority is running a dual system which combines both inclusive and non-inclusive approaches.

What Barnardo's is doing
Barnardo's is committed to the principle of inclusion for all children and works to overcome the barriers that prevent certain groups of children from access to schools and communities, while providing the necessary level of support to enable them to take part in mainstream society.

Our early years services aim to dismantle barriers to the participation of children with different physical and learning abilities. One family centre runs a playgroup and playschemes where children with some form of disability or developmental delay mix happily with other children of their own age, supported by a team of volunteers.

Other projects work with disabled children from birth through to adulthood to ensure that they have the same options throughout childhood as non-disabled children. The projects work with families and the local community to ensure that disabled children have access to education, health care and leisure facilities and the same opportunities to participate as everybody else.

We run parent partnership schemes, which support families with disabled children in the education system, providing information and advice, and working with families to ensure that the child has the best provision from the start and to prevent unnecessary conflict or dispute.

Barnardo's also provides services for children and young people with complex special educational needs in day and residential schools and units. Wherever possible, the projects aim to reintegrate children into mainstream schooling.

However, for some young people the severity of their emotional and behavioural problems means that they would be unlikely to benefit from returning to mainstream education as it stands currently and are best supported in a separate environment. These young people still follow the National Curriculum and interests in sport, drama, art and music are encouraged to help them develop confidence and social skills in preparation for adult life.

References
1. Office of National Statistics, *Social Trends 30*, Stationery Office, 2000
2. *Transition to adulthood*, Barnardo's, 1996
3. C Parsons and K Howlett *Difficult dilemmas*, Education 22 Dec 1995
4. *NCH Factfile 2000*, NCH Action for Children, 1999
5. Norwich, B *Segregation and inclusion: English LEA statistics 1988-1992*, Centre for Studies on Inclusive Education, 1994
6. OFSTED, *Special needs and the national curriculum*, HMSO, 1993
7. J Sebba with D Sachdev, *What works in inclusive education?* Barnardo's, 1997
8. Adult Commission, *Getting in on the Act*, HMSO, 1992

• The above information is from a Barnardo's briefing. See page 41 for their address details.

Learning disabilities

Information from the Department of Health

Facts and figures

The majority of people with learning disabilities have always lived in the community. At one time it was thought that those who could not be cared for at home should be placed in institutions. Whether a person lived at home or in an institution they often found themselves segregated from the rest of society.

A Royal Commission which reported in 1957 recommended radical changes with a new emphasis on community care and breaking down segregation. The 1971 White Paper 'Better Services for the Mentally Handicapped' and the Education (Handicapped Children) Act 1970, which gave a right to education, added impetus to these changes. A review followed in 1980 which led to the document *Progress, Problems and Priorities*. In 1992 the Department issued the circular *Social Care for Adults With Learning Disabilities*. The emphasis has been increasingly on arranging services in ways which meet individual needs and enable each person to develop their full potential.

(England only) A number of epidemiological studies suggests there are around 160,000 adults with severe and profound learning disabilities most of whom are living initially in their family homes and later on in appropriate residential accommodation. Research also suggests that between 0.45% and 0.6% of children will have a moderate to severe learning disability.

This suggests that there are between 55,000 and 75,000 children with a moderate to severe learning disability, the majority of whom live at home with one or two parents.

Services

• The number of people under the learning disability specialty in NHS hospitals and units in 1999 was over 7,000.
• The number of residential care places for people with learning disabilities in 1999 was over 51,000.
• The number of day centre places provided or purchased during a sample week in 1998 was over 283,000.

Expenditure

A total of almost £3bn is spent on services for people with learning disabilities (amount is split fairly evenly between health and social care).

In 2000/2001 the Department awarded grants totalling nearly £1.3m to the learning disability voluntary sector under the Section 64 General Scheme which encourages policy development and the spread of good practice.

13 grants were awarded to assist with organisations' core administrative costs and 23 grants for innovative project work.

Time to open a new set of doors

Under a new Bill, schools must meet the requirements of pupils with special needs. Sarah Cassidy asks if inclusive education can really work

When Adam Field finished junior school, he had his heart set on a place at the secondary school near his home in Eastbourne, where his friends were going.

But Adam, now 14, was diagnosed with a bone disorder when he was four which has affected his joints and means he now has to use a wheelchair. He could still walk when he finished primary school but his parents knew he would soon need a wheelchair, and that they had to choose a school that would be able to accommodate it.

'The local secondary school had no lifts, no special facilities, no anything,' says Adam. 'It would have been very difficult for me to get around.'

He is now a pupil at Filsham Valley School, a mainstream school in St Leonards, East Sussex, where he is one of 55 students with severe physical or sensory impairments supported by a special centre within the school.

'When I first came to the school, I really did not want to be here. It's quite a long way from home, I have to come in a taxi, and I wanted to be with my friends in Eastbourne,' he says. 'But there is much better access here – I can get around everywhere on my own and do much more. Now I'm settled, I am enjoying it.'

His mother Marian was delighted and relieved when Adam got a place at Filsham Valley – one of just seven available that year. 'Adam has always been very independent. There's nothing wrong with him mentally. I just wanted him to be as normal as possible,' she says. 'We would never have sent him to a special school – he's going to have to go out into the world and fend for himself, and we wanted him to mix with children in a mainstream school.

'If he hadn't got a place at Filsham Valley, I don't know what we would have done. No other local school could cope with a wheelchair. A lot more needs to be done for children with disabilities.'

> **'We are educating a new generation who will not just treat people with special needs as equals, but will not think of them as particularly special or different'**

Increasing numbers of schools will soon have to reassess their attitudes to children like Adam, when the Special Education Needs and Disability Bill becomes law next September.

The Bill will strengthen the right of pupils with special needs to attend a mainstream school, if that is what their parents want. It will make it more difficult for schools to refuse pupils on the grounds that they cannot cope with their disability. Once the Bill is in place, schools will only be able to refuse a child with a special need a place if admitting him or her would harm the education of the other pupils. By putting education within the remit of the Disability Discrimination Act for the first time, the Bill will also make it illegal to discriminate against a student because of his or her disability.

At Filsham Valley, children with serious medical conditions such as muscular dystrophy, spina bifida and cystic fibrosis are taught alongside mainstream pupils, as well as blind students and children with Asperger's – a mild form of autism. Many take time out of mainstream lessons for physiotherapy, speech therapy or extra classes in literacy, numeracy and social skills. But all spend most of their time in mainstream classes.

Deputy head teacher Helen Kenward believes that most schools easily accept students with dis-

abilities, without significant extra resources. She accepts that her school is lucky to have the specialist centre based at the school, but adds: 'It is about how resourceful you are, not just what resources you have. A lot of it is about attitude, and whether staff really want a special needs child in their class. If the school wants to take a child, there is not really anything stopping them.'

Richard Rieser, director of the charity Disability Equality in Education, is working with schools and colleges to train staff in preparation for the reforms. He believes that only 1 or 2 per cent of the country's 24,000 schools are ready to cope with the changes brought by the Bill.

'The Bill will mean real change for many schools,' he says. 'Historically, some schools have simply taken on inclusion, but even more have not. They have just told parents of a child with special needs, "we can't take you, but we know a school down the road that can", so there has been a clustering effect. The old idea was that the child with special needs had a problem. The solution was to diagnose the problem and support the child in order to cope with it. The new way of thinking starts from the premise that every child has the right to attend their local school. The school must look to see what are the barriers that are keeping that child out, and work to remove them.'

The Bill is welcomed by supporters of 'inclusive education' as a step in the right direction. But many teachers and parents are concerned that it could mean more children with very challenging behaviour being allowed into mainstream classrooms. This Easter, the teaching unions voiced their concerns about inclusion at their annual conferences by voting to refuse to teach aggressive children.

Nigel de Gruchy, general secretary of the National Association of Schoolmasters/Union of Women Teachers, fears that inclusion is creating an excessive workload for teachers. 'There are still not enough resources going into schools to support these children,' he says. 'Even when the resources are available, having extra support staff in the

classroom creates an extra workload and stresses for teachers.

'When it comes to bad behaviour and children with emotional and behavioural difficulties, you can forget it. It can work, but very often it just disrupts the education of the rest of the class.'

But Mr Rieser argues that only a minority of children with special needs display challenging behaviour. He says that inclusion will mean a dramatic change in the role of teachers. 'Rather than being the only adult in charge of a class, there will be two or three adults supporting children with high levels of need. The teacher will become the team leader, rather than the lone practitioner. There are benefits to the other children of having four adults in the class rather than one.'

Ms Kenward believes that the climate is already changing. 'I think schools will have to take notice of [the Bill]. It will make people think about what children with special needs need in school.

'Having children with disabilities in the class takes away the mystique of it. We are educating a new generation who will not just treat people with special needs as equals, but will not think of them as particularly special or different.'

What the students say

Charlie Piper, 13, has cerebral palsy and is in a wheelchair
'At my previous school I could get around the whole school but I had to go outside and right round the school to get to some classrooms. If it was raining someone would have to come and carry me.

'At Filsham Valley I can go everywhere on my own and there are quite a few people in wheelchairs so I fit in more – but I also have the chance to mix with everyone else.'

Jade Welch, 13
'Before we started at Filsham Valley I thought it might be a bit strange having Charlie in the class. I knew who she was because we'd been to the same playgroup but had been to different primary schools so I didn't know her very well.

'I was a bit worried about how I would talk to her if she was down in her chair and everyone else was standing up. But it turned out to be OK. It was only strange for a couple of days.

'Charlie's a good friend to me. She's got a great personality and that's all that matters really.

'I'm glad that she's in my lessons. I don't think it would be fair if she wasn't allowed to be in the classroom just because she's in a wheelchair.'

What the law says
Special Educational Needs and Disability Bill:

- Strengthens the rights of children with special educational needs to a place at a mainstream school.

    Puts education within the remit of the Disability Discrimination Act.

- Places a new duty on local education authorities to establish independent panels to prevent and resolve disputes.

- Requires schools and colleges to make reasonable adjustments to their policies and practices.

- Requires the post-16 sector to make physical changes to their premises to improve access and to provide extra services for pupils with special needs.

- Requires local education authorities and schools to improve access for disabled pupils to premises, to the curriculum and to written information.

From September 2001: most of the special educational needs provisions.
- From September 2002: all schools and post-16 disability duties.
- September 2003: duty to provide aids and services for post-16s.
- September 2005: alter or remove features in post-16 where disabled students are disadvantaged.

The neglect of so many disabled pupils is scandalous

Today's report on the plight of the UK's 22,000 blind and partially sighted young has a special resonance for David Blunkett, the country's first blind Cabinet minister. Mr Blunkett, who attended special schools for the blind, knows all about the misery of confining children with special needs to educational ghettos. He has been a passionate supporter of a policy that brings such children into mainstream schools, where it is practical. No wonder he was angry when he read the report from the Royal National Institute for the Blind.

For the Institute's survey reveals the scandalous neglect of blind young people in mainstream schools. What conceivable reason is there for not giving a quarter of visually-impaired secondary pupils handouts in large print or Braille, or excluding them from some courses? Universities are even worse, with only half the students getting materials they need in the right format.

The report exposes the potential dangers of the Government's policy of encouraging mainstream schooling for growing numbers of pupils – not just blind pupils, but all those with learning difficulties. It is right that every effort should be made to give children the chance of education in an ordinary school, but both schools and ministers have to face up to the consequences. Mr Blunkett is pumping more money into schools to help them to adapt to the needs of pupils with disabilities. Training teachers to be more sensitive to these children is also a matter of urgency. The story of Simon Cruden, whose teachers didn't want to know after he became blind, is horrifying.

A Bill due to be announced in the Queen's Speech is expected to strengthen the rights of special-needs pupils by extending to children the rights already enjoyed by adults under the Disability Discrimination Act. New advocates will help parents in their lonely struggle to force local education authorities to pay for the help these children so desperately need.

It is right that every effort should be made to give children the chance of education in an ordinary school

---

Mr Blunkett must not let down all those children currently being failed by the education system. When he leaves his present post, children with special needs must have stronger support than they have now. But changes in the law will not by themselves guarantee that cases like those of Simon Cruden do not recur, or that others like him receive the simple, practical support that they should expect in any civilised society. Ministers must remain vigilant.

© 2001 The Independent Newspaper (UK) Ltd

'It is not disability but an attitude problem of others'

By Steve Connor

Alistair Wright is the severely deaf father of a six-year-old son who has normal hearing. Mr Wright, a single parent, aged 33, works for the National Deaf Children's Society which brings him into contact with many deaf parents and their children. He also has a deaf sister who has children of her own.

Any genetic test that can help to diagnose deafness in babies at an early age would be welcomed, Mr Wright said. But such tests should never be used to alienate deaf people in society. 'Naturally, I am concerned at the possibility of it being used for "cleansing" of deaf children but it can be a great tool in early diagnosis for hearing parents in order to prepare all the support for their deaf child,' he said.

'For hearing parents, the earlier they know if their child is diagnosed as being deaf will be an enormous help in their preparation for having a deaf child. It will enable them to be aware of the audiological, communication, language, educational and social issues which approximately 90 per cent of parents will know very little about,' said Mr Wright.

Mr Wright went to a boarding school for deaf children and much of his social life is centred around deaf people. He believes that pre-implantation genetic diagnosis is unlikely to be used by many deaf people to ensure they have a deaf child, but neither would it be used to ensure they have a hearing child. He said: 'It is a hearing-oriented society and that will be helpful in bringing up hearing children for deaf parents. Being deaf with their own experiences will give them the skills required to bring up deaf children.

'Parents should not be under any pressure to have hearing-only children as deafness is not a disability but an attitude problem of others . . . Deaf children face a brighter future than those of the older deaf generations.'

© 2001 The Independent Newspaper (UK) Ltd

More money for disabled students

Colleges demand a bigger slice of the funding, reports Simon Midgley

Colleges will today plead that they should get more money than universities to improve access for the disabled because they serve more than twice as many students.

The special educational needs and disability bill, which gets its second Commons reading today, earmarks £20m for English colleges over the next two years.

This compares with £56m set aside for such spending in higher education institutions. While backing the new legislation, Judith Norrington, the Association of Colleges' director of curriculum and quality, said that in order for colleges to make learning accessible for as many disabled learners as possible more money would need to be found in the years to come.

'It's such a worthwhile purpose that we want to do it properly, and it needs to be effectively resourced. The current funding on offer would not meet total needs by any means and we would look for further support over future years.'

Ms Norrington said that further education – with more than 4m students in some 420 colleges in England compared to some 1.6m students in considerably fewer higher education institutions – deserved proportionately greater funding.

The thrust of the current bill is that the needs of disabled learners should be met wherever reasonable – that they should be entitled to access to buildings and places where they can learn.

Underpinning the legislation will be guidance to make sure people get learning support. There will also be regulated pre-16 and adult appeals processes and a greater emphasis on integrating disabled learners into mainstream education wherever possible.

The Association of Colleges is to draw up a list of things that each college will need to do to ensure access. This will also lead to some sense of what costs are likely to be involved.

Some years ago the Further Education Funding Council did a survey in one region of England to see what kind of costs could be involved in improving accessibility by introducing lifts and ramps, etc. Ms Norrington says that extrapolating from this figure suggests a national bill of some £150m.

The funding council is keen that work-based training providers should be required to make the same improvements to accessibility as colleges, under the same regulatory regime. And in the same way organisations offering students work placements should also have to take reasonable steps to support disabled learning.

At present the legislation emphasises that individuals must make it clear that they are disabled or have special educational needs. However the association wants to make it a joint responsibility with colleges to find out whether an individual has a disability or needs help.

© Guardian Newspapers Limited 2001

Understanding learning disability

People who have been labelled as mentally handicapped do not like it, and many prefer to be described as having learning disabilities or special needs. They feel that these terms communicate better the difficulties they face and the needs they have in learning to live in a complex and often uncaring society.

Mental disability (handicap) is sometimes confused with mental illness, though they are very different. A person who is diagnosed as mentally ill can temporarily hold a distorted view of the world as a result of their feelings of distress. A person with learning disabilities may seem to have a very individual view of the world, but it is consistent and stable.

What causes it?

There are many different causes of learning disability, some of them unknown. Damage to the brain may be caused by inherited factors, or may result from injury during the birth process, illness or accident.

About one baby in every 1000 has Down's Syndrome. The most common form of learning disability, Down's Syndrome is a genetic condition caused by the presence of an extra chromosome. Only 1 per cent of people with Down's Syndrome have inherited the condition. In general it arises as a result of a genetic accident from parents with a completely 'normal' genetic make-up.

In other cases a child's brain may be damaged during birth – for example, if for some reason the supply of blood to the baby's brain gets restricted for a period of time. An adverse reaction to a vaccination can also cause damage to the brain, as can an illness such as meningitis, and a serious accidental injury to the head.

• The above information is an extract of MIND's booklet *Understanding Learning Disability*. To obtain a copy contact MIND at the address on page 41.

© MIND

Special Educational Needs and Disability Bill

By Sophie Corlett, Policy Director – Higher Education

The Special Educational Needs and Disability Act became law on 11 May 2001. As a result, discrimination against disabled students in the provision of education, training and other related services will become unlawful. The legislation will apply in England, Wales and Scotland but not, as yet, in Northern Ireland.

The new Act covers pre- and post-16 education, but the following article deals only with post-16 issues.

Who will the Act protect?

The new Act is an amendment to the existing Disability Discrimination Act 1995 (DDA), and therefore only protects people who are defined as disabled according to that legislation. This is not ideal, because the definition of disability in the DDA is based on an individual's ability to carry out 'normal day-to-day' activities. So, for example, 'inability to concentrate on a task requiring application over several hours' is not considered disabling, because concentration over a long period, however common for students taking exams, is not considered to be a 'normal' day-to-day activity. It seems likely, therefore, that there will be a number of people who will not be able to use the new legislation. However, many of these students will continue to be provided for by the support systems within their institutions, and will continue to be eligible for Disabled Students' Allowances and other assistance.

Who will have responsibilities under the new law?

The new law will give new responsibilities to all further and higher education institutions, schools with post-16 provision (although these are covered by the pre-16 sections of the Act, not the post-16 sections), and local authorities when these organisations provide further, adult or continuing education or training that is funded or partially funded through one of the funding councils, Learning and Skills Council, National Council for Education and Training in Wales or an education authority. The statutory youth service is also covered. The Act also allows for regulations to designate more institutions as being covered by the legislation, and it is understood that many specialist residential colleges for disabled people will be brought under the provisions in this way. Work-based training providers are not covered by the new legislation and will continue to be covered by Part III of the DDA.

What does the Act cover?

The new law will affect all education and training provided by these bodies, admissions to courses, exclusions, and the provision of other 'student services'. 'Student services' is an all-inclusive term, and includes services of any description provided wholly or mainly for students or those enrolled on courses. This includes not only education, but residential accommodation, leisure facilities, catering and library facilities, careers and welfare services, and services already covered by Part III of the existing DDA. These services will transfer from Part III of the DDA to the new provisions as these come into force.

What will education providers have to do?

It will be unlawful for institutions or other education providers to treat a disabled person 'less favourably' than they treat, or would treat non-disabled people for a reason which relates to the person's disability. For example, it would be unlawful for an institution to turn a disabled person away from a course, or mark them down in an assessment, because they had dyslexia or were deaf.

Part of not discriminating is making 'adjustments'. If a disabled person is at a 'substantial disadvantage', the education provider is required to take such steps as are reasonable to prevent that

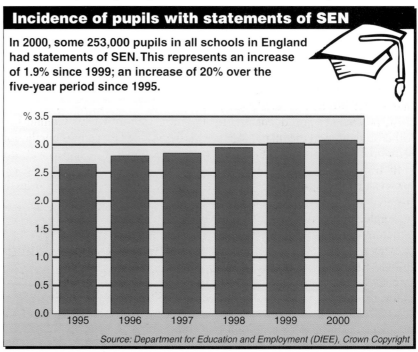

Incidence of pupils with statements of SEN

In 2000, some 253,000 pupils in all schools in England had statements of SEN. This represents an increase of 1.9% since 1999; an increase of 20% over the five-year period since 1995.

Source: Department for Education and Employment (DfEE), Crown Copyright

disadvantage. This might include changes to policies and practices, changes to course requirements or work placements, changes to physical features of a building, the provision of interpreters or other support workers, the delivery of courses in alternative ways, or the provision of materials in other formats.

For those services already required to make reasonable adjustments under Part III, this will be familiar territory. However, it is worth noting that the threshold for adjustments (when existing arrangements place a disabled person at a 'substantial disadvantage') is much lower than for Part III (when arrangements are 'impossible or unreasonably difficult to access').

The concept of adjustments will also require educators to look at some fundamental issues regarding their academic/subject disciplines and the methods used to teach and assess these. It is not expected that academic standards should be lowered to accommodate disabled students – one of the justifications for less favourable treatment, and one of the criteria for determining whether or not an adjustment is 'reasonable', will be the maintenance of academic or other relevant course standards. However, it will not be enough for institutions to use this defence without thinking through the implications. They will need to consider what is essential to these subjects, and so cannot be compromised, and what is peripheral or incidental and so can be waived or substituted.

Besides academic standards, the reasonableness of individual adjustments can also be measured against cost, practicality and disruption to other students and the financial and other resources available. Providers will not be expected to replicate provision which students already receive through other means, for example, support funded by disabled students' allowances. They may, however, need to think about providing appropriate access to those groups of students ineligible for such allowances.

The duty to make reasonable adjustments is a duty to disabled people generally, not just to

particular individuals. This 'anticipatory' aspect effectively means that providers must consider what sort of adjustments may be necessary for disabled people in the future, and where appropriate make adjustments in advance.

The anticipatory nature of the legislation should mean that the needs of some disabled students will be met automatically. In other cases, adjustments will need to be made for individuals in response to particular needs. There will thus be a responsibility on education providers to do what they can to find out whether individuals have disability-related needs. However, if an education provider has made reasonable attempts to find out, but an individual student has chosen not to disclose their disability or need, education providers will not be liable for any failure to make specific individual adjustments.

Redress

The Disability Rights Commission is being asked to set up a conciliation service, which it is hoped will deal with most complaints in a speedy and effective way. If both parties do

not agree to conciliation, or if conciliation fails, students may take cases to court (the county court in England and Wales and the sheriff court in Scotland). Courts will have the power not only to determine the rights of the case, but also award compensation and impose injunctions or interdicts to ensure discriminatory practices are reviewed.

Timetable

With two exceptions, the new legislation will be in force by 1 September 2002. The exceptions are reasonable adjustments involving the provision of auxiliary aids and services (such as interpreters etc.) which comes into force on 1 September 2003 and the requirement to make physical adjustments which is to be implemented on 1 September 2005.

Skill is working with the Disability Rights Commission to produce a statutory Code of Practice which will provide guidance to providers on the implementation of the new law. The Code is out for consultation until October 2001, and will be published in final form in March 2002.

• The above information is an extract from Skill's factsheet *Special Educational Needs and Disability Bill*, which is available from their web site at www.skill.org.uk Alternatively, see page 41 for their address details.

© Skill: National Bureau for Students with Disabililties

> *The anticipatory nature of the legislation should mean that the needs of some disabled students will be met automatically*

Scotland puts learning disabilities centre stage

By David Mitchell

Services for people with learning disabilities in Scotland have taken a giant leap forward with plans to set up a Scottish development centre for learning disabilities.

A consortium of 13 organisations, led by charity Enable, has been awarded £1.5m over five years to develop the Glasgow-based centre, which will be up and running by September to offer advice, training and support to agencies, professionals and people with learning disabilities.

But despite the jubilation over the centre's go-ahead, there is still widespread concern that not enough is being done to implement the Scottish executive's 10-year blueprint for services, unveiled last May, which originally suggested the centre.

The strategic review, *The Same as You?*, set a deadline for closing all long-stay hospitals by 2005; proposed a change fund to help councils and health boards implement it, and promised direct payments to allow people to buy their own services by 2003.

So far the executive has failed to produce an implementation plan; local authorities and health boards have had to wait for guidance on local partnership agreements, and there are fears the change fund will not be enough.

Norman Dunning, director of Enable, said: 'The process has taken a lot longer than expected, but now at least we have got the centre, which is a start. The executive has been dragging its feet – it should have got this sorted out a lot quicker and produced an action plan.

'We are also disappointed at the size of the change fund – £36m over three years – which seems wholly inadequate. It's being distributed to authorities as part of their general grant allocation, so there is no guarantee it will be spent on people with learning disabilities, let alone the review. It is absolutely crazy.'

As well as providing consultancy, training and advice, the new centre will gather information on needs and services; provide education materials; promote public education, and disseminate latest research. In line with the review, it will be user and carer-led, with at least half of its board of trustees made up of users or carers.

Malcolm Matheson, director of consortium member Key Housing Association, which provides supported accommodation for 800 people with learning disabilities throughout Scotland, sees this as of crucial importance.

'As the policy was being developed, the people we support expressed a very clear view that the strategy and the centre should be fully inclusive and have people with learning disabilities and their carers at the heart. Our aim is to try and support people with learning disabilities to do that and become a driving force behind this initiative,' he said.

'But the centre is not going to be the answer to everything and there is disappointment that the impetus for the review seems to have gone. The key players at the Scottish executive who worked on the strategy have been moved to other activities and the implementation is not as well resourced as it should be.'

> **'People have been neglected in the past. Hopefully, the centre will eventually change the way people work and help make society a lot better'**

James Hogg, professor of profound disabilities at Dundee University – one of four universities in the consortium – said the new centre would, for the first time, provide a focus for the activities of everyone working in the field.

'We hope to set up a wider group of universities in which anyone carrying out research can collaborate with us, providing an expert resource to draw on. But the executive needs to produce guidance on various aspects of implementing the review. The sooner we have that, the easier the task will be for people working at local level,' he said.

For Idem Lewis, who has a learning disability and is a tenants' adviser for Key Housing, the centre means people with learning disabilities will be taking an active part in its running, whereas in the past it would have been professionals with little contact with service users.

'It is important to remember that when care in the community was launched in the early 1990s, the decision makers didn't think of how it was not just about putting people into houses, but about looking at communities and how people were discriminated against,' he said.

'People have been neglected in the past. Hopefully, the centre will eventually change the way people work and help make society a lot better by leading on courses, research and public education. It will make a big difference.'

The executive said progress was being made and guidance had been issued to councils and health boards on local partnership agreements.

'We have also set out proposals in the long-term care bill for consultation on direct payments and, locally, agencies are making progress on hospital retractions, joint services and resourcing, improved advocacy and alternatives to traditional day services,' said a spokeswoman.

ADDITIONAL RESOURCES

You might like to contact the following organisations for further information. Due to the increasing cost of postage, many organisations cannot respond to enquiries unless they receive a stamped, addressed envelope.

Barnardo's
Tanners Lane, Barkingside
Ilford, Essex, IG6 1QG
Tel: 020 8550 8822
Fax: 020 8551 6870
E-mail: media.team@barnardos.org.uk
Web site: www.barnardos.org.uk
Barnardo's helps children, young people and their families over the long term to overcome the most severe disadvantages – problems like disability, abuse, homelessness and poverty.

British Institute of Learning Disabilities (BILD)
Wolverhampton Road
Kidderminster
Worcestershire, DY10 3PP
Tel: 01562 850251
Fax: 01562 851970
E-mail: bild@bild.demon.co.uk
Web site: www.bild.org.uk
BILD publishes a series of high quality journals designed to keep you up to date with innovation and best practice in learning disability.

Disabled Drivers' Association
Ashwellthorpe
Norwich, NR16 1EX
Tel: 01508 489449
Fax: 01508 418173
E-mail: ddahq@aol.com
Web site: www.dda.org.uk
Assists and encourages disabled people towards independence through greater mobility. Produces the publication *Magic Carpet*.

Disabled Living Foundation (DLF)
380-384 Harrow Road
London, W9 2HU
Tel: 020 7289 6111
Fax: 020 7266 2922
E-mail: info@dlf.org.uk
Web site: www.dlf.org.uk
Gives advice and information on any aspect of ordinary life presenting problems and difficulties to people of all ages with any disability. Helpline 0845 130 9177. Opening hours 10am-4pm, Monday to Friday.

The Employers' Forum on Disability
Nutmeg House
60 Gainsford Street
London, SE1 2NY
Tel: 020 7403 3020
Fax: 020 7403 0404
Web site: www.employers-forum.co.uk
The Employers' Forum on Disability is the national employers' organisation focused on disability in the UK.

The Foundation for People with Learning Disabilities
20/21 Cornwall Terrace
London, NW1 4QL
Tel: 020 7535 7400
Fax: 020 7535 7474
E-mail: fpld@fpld.org.uk
Web site: www.learningdisabilities.org.uk
The Foundation is a registered charity, part of the Mental Health Foundation. They work with people with learning disabilities to improve the quality of their lives.

The Industrial Society
Customer Centre
49 Calthorpe Road
Edgbaston
Birmingham, B15 1TH
Tel: 01870 400 1000
Fax: 01780 400 1099
Produces range of booklets and information packs on all sorts of work related issues including: working mothers, racial and sexual harasment, and disabilities.

Leonard Cheshire
Leonard Cheshire House
30 Millbank
London, SW1P 4QD
Tel: 020 7802 8200
Fax: 020 7802 8250
E-mail: info@london.leonard-cheshire.org.uk
Web site: www.leonard-cheshire.org
Provides a range of care services for people with physical or learning disabilities and those with mental health problems. Produces publications.

MIND
Granta House, 15-19 Broadway
Stratford, London, E15 4BQ
Tel: 020 8519 2122
Fax: 020 8522 1725
E-mail: contact@mind.org.uk
Web site: www.mind.org.uk
For a full publications list send a stamped addressed envelope to Mind Mail Order, 15-19 Broadway, London E15 4BQ.

National Citizens' Advice Bureaux
Myddleton House
115-123 Pentonville
London, N1 9LZ
Tel: 020 7833 2181
Fax: 020 7833 4367
Web site: www.nacab.org.uk
For free and confidential advice search the CAB directory for your nearest bureau.

Royal Association for Disability and Rehabilitation (RADAR)
12 City Forum, 250 City Road
London, EC1V 8AF
Tel: 020 7250 3222
Fax: 020 7250 0212
E-mail: radar@radar.org.uk
Web site: www.radar.org.uk
RADAR is a national organisation of and for disabled people. It campaigns for improvements in disabled people's lives.

Skill: National Bureau for Students with Disabililties
Chapter House
18-20 Crucifix Lane
London, SE1 3JW
Tel: 020 7450 0620
Fax: 020 7450 0650
E-mail: admin@skill.org.uk
Web site: www.skill.org.uk
Skill promotes opportunities for young people and adults with any kind of disability in post-16 education, training and employment across the UK. Runs an information service voice: 0800 328 5050 (freephone); voice: 020 7657 2337; text: 0800 068 2422 (freetext).

INDEX

abuse, of people with learning disabilities 30
advertising, and disabled people 12
age discrimination, and disability benefits 7

babies, diagnosing deafness in 36
benefits (State), disability benefits 7-9, 20
blind children 36
boys and young men, with learning disabilities 30

cancer, and employment rights 19
carers, support for 26-7
child poverty, and disability 10
children
    blind 36
    deaf 36
    with special needs 10, 26, 31-2, 34-6, 38

deaf people
    children 36
    and shopping 6
disability benefits 7-9
    attendance allowance (AA) 7, 9
    and care needs 8, 9
    disability living allowance (DLA) 7, 8-9
    disabled persons tax credit 7
    incapacity benefit 7, 20
    and mobility needs 8
Disability Discrimination Act 1, 2, 14-15, 19, 23, 27
    and special educational needs 35, 36, 38
Disability Movement 3
Disability Rights Commission 1, 2, 39
Disabled Living Foundation (DLF) 3-5
disabled people
    and accessibility 5
        Left Out campaign 22-3
    attitudes to 1, 5, 11-12, 25
    and communication difficulties 4
    cultural and social influences on disability 4-5
    defining disability 3-4, 17
        administrative model of 4
        charitable model of 4
        medical model of 3, 25-6
        social model of 3-4, 12, 26
    and disability awareness 1, 3-5
    and the Disability Rights Commission 1
    and discrimination see discrimination, disabled people
    employment see employment, of disabled people
    facts and figures 1, 3
    and families/carers 26
    and financial security 5
    hidden disabilities 4
    language used to describe 11-12, 25
    and the media 12
    numbers of 25
    parking for 21, 22, 23
    and physical impairment 4
    rights of 13

    and sensory impairment 4
    and shopping 6, 23
    types of impairment 4
    in the UK, facts and figures 10
    see also disability benefits; learning disabilities
discrimination
    disabled people
        and access to facilities 22, 25
        and conciliation 2
        defining 2
        and education 26
        and employment 15, 19, 20-1, 26, 27
        goods and services 26, 27
        and shopping 6, 23, 26
        speaking publicly about 2
        see also Disability Discrimination Act
Down's syndrome 30, 37

education
    and the Special Educational Needs and Disability Bill
        34-5, 36, 38-9
    see also schools
employment
    of disabled people 14-20
        access to the workplace 14, 21
        attitudes to 11, 15, 16
        best practice guidelines 15
        in the Civil Service 17
        and the Disability Discrimination Act 14, 15, 27
        and disability rights 19
        and discrimination 5, 15, 19, 20-1, 26
        facts and figures 14, 20
        local authority schemes and sheltered workshops 16
        management strategies 18-19
        and productivity 20
        and the structure of the working day 5
        and Welfare to Work measures 14
    of people with learning disabilities 29, 30

families, and disabled people, support for 5, 26-7
further education, and disabled students 37

genes, and disability 4
Government policies, on disabled people 14, 20, 21

HIV (human immunodeficiency virus), and employment
    rights 19
human rights, and disabled people 13

incomes, low incomes and disability 4

learning disabilities 4, 28-40
    abuse of people with 30
    characteristics of people with 28, 29
    Down's syndrome 30, 37
    and employment 29, 30
    facts and figures 33
    global terminology 29
    medical treatment for people with 30

and mental illness 29, 37
    mild 28, 30
    numbers of people with 29, 30
    organisations 28-9
    services for people with
        care facilities 33
        expenditure on 33
        in Scotland 40
    severe 28, 30
    understanding 37
lifestyle, as a cause of disability 4
local authorities
    and children with special needs 32
    and disabled people 16

media, and disabled people 12
mental illness 4
    and learning disabilities 29, 37

parents, of children with special needs 33
poverty
    child poverty and disability 10
    and disability benefits 7
    and people with learning disabilities 30
prejudice, and disabled people 11, 12
public attitudes, to disabled people 1

schools, and disabled/special needs children 10, 26, 31-2, 34-6
shopping, and disabled customers 6, 23

special needs children 10, 26, 31-2, 34-6, 38
special schools 26

teachers, and special needs children 35
transport
    and disabled drivers 24
        and car parking 21, 22, 23

United Nations (UN), and disabled people 13
universities, and disabled students 37

visually impaired people
    and barriers to ability 5
    and employment rights 19

wheelchair users
    access to amenities 5
    assumptions made about 11
    and employment discrimination 20-1
    and impairment 4
    numbers of 1
    schools for 34, 35
    and shopping 6
    and transport 24
women, with learning disabilities 30
workplace discrimination, and disabled people 5, 15, 19, 20-1

young people
    disabled students 37
    with learning disabilities 30, 33

* * * * *

The Internet has been likened to shopping in a supermarket without aisles. The press of a button on a web browser can bring up thousands of sites but working your way through them to find what you want can involve long and frustrating on-line searches.

And unfortunately many sites contain inaccurate, misleading or heavily biased information. Our researchers have therefore undertaken an extensive analysis to bring you a selection of quality web site addresses.

Skill: National Bureau for Students with Disabililties
www.skill.org.uk

This is a good web site for students with disabilities, or those wanting information on disability issues. By clicking on Information you will find such things as Frequently Asked Questions, Information Sheets, Publications, News, Policy, and an option to search for information sheets relevant to your circumstances.

Disability NOW
www.disabilitynow.org.uk

One of the UK's leading disability sites, giving a whole range of useful information, news and feature articles. Click on the Links button to find a scroll list of areas of disabilities, each one giving a list of dozens of UK web sites.

SCOPE
www.scope.org.uk

From the home page there is a link to Factsheets and Publications. Under the factsheet option there is a listing including An Introduction to Disability Issue. There is also a lot of information on cerebral palsy and Education and conductive education – you can download some in PDF format.

The Foundation for People with Learning Disabilities
www.learningdisabilities.org.uk

From the home page there is a link to The Issues on which there is a listing of options including Introduction, Basic Information, Rights and Values and Someone to talk to – a list of organisations which can help if you or someone you support has a learning disability.

ACKNOWLEDGEMENTS

The publisher is grateful for permission to reproduce the following material.

While every care has been taken to trace and acknowledge copyright, the publisher tenders its apology for any accidental infringement or where copyright has proved untraceable. The publisher would be pleased to come to a suitable arrangement in any such case with the rightful owner.

Chapter One: Discrimination

In the dark on disability, © Guardian Newspapers Limited 2001, *What is discrimination?*, © Disability Rights Commission, *Disability awareness*, © Disabled Living Foundation (DLF), *Disabled customers*, © The Employers' Forum on Disability, *Poverty and benefits*, © Disability Daily, *Disability Living Allowance*, © Crown copyright is reproduced with the permission of the Controller of Her Majesty's Stationery Office (HMSO), *Benefits for the extra costs of disability*, © National Association of Citizens' Advice Bureaux, *Attendance Allowance*, © Crown copyright is reproduced with the permission of the Controller of Her Majesty's Stationery Office (HMSO), *Disabled children*, © Disability Daily, *Disability in the UK*, © The Employers' Forum on Disability, *Talking my language*, © Leonard Cheshire, 2001, *A role for the disabled*, © Telegraph Group Limited, London 2000, *Human wrongs*, © Guardian Newspapers Limited 2001, *Disability discrimination*, © The Industrial Society, *Regional disabled people still excluded from work*, © Leonard Cheshire, 2001, *Call to give disabled real job opportunities*, © Guardian Newspapers Limited 2001, *Disability does not mean inability*, © 2001 The Independent Newspaper (UK) Ltd, *Employment*, © RADAR, *Disabled people in the labour market*, © Crown copyright is reproduced with the permission of the Controller of Her Majesty's Stationery Office (HMSO), *Disability rights to cover millions more workers*, © Guardian Newspapers Limited 2001, *Disabled people as workers*, © The Employers' Forum on Disability, *Disabled people and society*, © 2001 Independent Newspaper (UK) Ltd, *Left out*, © Scope, *What are the characteristics of disabled drivers?*, © RAC, *And the survey shows . . .* , © The Disabled Drivers' Association, *Use of public transport*, © RAC, *Disability issues*, © Scope.

Chapter Two: Learning Disabilities

What is a learning disability?, © The Foundation for People with Learning Disabilities, *Learning disabilities*, © Crown copyright is reproduced with the permission of the Controller of Her Majesty's Stationery Office (HMSO), *British Institute of Learning Disabilities*, © British Institute of Learning Disabilities, *How many people have learning disabilities?*, © The Foundation for People with Learning Disabilities, *Mencap research points to the public's double standards*, © 2001 The Independent Newspaper (UK) Ltd, *Inclusive education*, © Barnardo's, *Numbers of children with disabilities*, © Crown copyright is reproduced with the permission of the Controller of Her Majesty's Stationery Office (HMSO), *Learning disabilities*, © Crown copyright is reproduced with the permission of the Controller of Her Majesty's Stationery Office (HMSO), *Time to open a new set of doors*, © 2001 The Independent Newspaper (UK) Ltd, *The neglect of so many disabled pupils is scandalous*, © 2001 The Independent Newspaper (UK) Ltd, *'It is not disability but an attitude problem of others'*, © 2001 The Independent Newspaper (UK) Ltd, *More money for disabled students*, © Guardian Newspapers Limited 2001, *Understanding learning disability*, © MIND, *Special Educational Needs and Disability Bill*, © Skill: National Bureau for Students with Disabilities, *Scotland puts learning disabilities centre stage*, © Guardian Newspapers Limited 2001.

Photographs and illustrations:

Pages 1, 6, 11, 14, 21, 25, 34: Simon Kneebone, pages 3, 5, 23, 39: Pumpkin House.

Craig Donnellan
Cambridge
September, 2001